THE GOSPEL

THE LIFE OF JESUS CHRIST

As Written By
Matthew, Mark, Luke, and John

Mary Jane Grubbs

WESTBOW°
PRESS
A DIVISION OF THOMAS NELSON
& ZONDERVAN

Scripture quotations taken from the New American Standard Bible˚, Copyright © 1960, 1962, 1963, 1968, 1971, 1972, 1973, 1975, 1977, 1995 by The Lockman Foundation. Used by permission. (www.Lockman.org)

WestBow Press books may be ordered through booksellers or by contacting:

WestBow Press
A Division of Thomas Nelson & Zondervan
1663 Liberty Drive
Bloomington, IN 47403
www.westbowpress.com
1 (866) 928-1240

ISBN: 978-1-4908-5921-7 (sc)
ISBN: 978-1-4908-5928-6 (e)

Library of Congress Control Number: 2014919919

Printed in the United States of America.

WestBow Press rev. date: 11/05/2014

DEDICATIONS

To my Savior for His Inspiration, Patience and Love.

To my parents Delbert and Phyllis Grubbs for
teaching me the love of Jesus Christ.

To Wanda Kunkel, my friend and Christian Mentor.

PROLOGUE

The book of Matthew was written by Matthew who was a tax collector. He became one of Jesus' disciples. The book is dated around A.D. 66. This book was written as a eyewitness account.

The book of Mark was written by John Mark, a companion of Peter who was one of Jesus' disciples. The book is dated around A.D. 65. This book was written by Mark as an observation of Peter's eyewitness preaching.

The book of Luke was written by Luke who was a physician. Luke was a follower of Paul who was an apostle. The book is dated around A.D. 58. This book was written by Luke as an observation of Paul's teachings.

The book of John was written by John who was a fisherman. He became one of Jesus' disciples. The book is dated around A.D.87. This book was written as a eyewitness account.

John 10:16

I have other sheep, which are not of this fold:
I must bring them also, and they shall hear My
voice; and they shall become one flock with
one Shepherd.

The word GOSPEL literally means "God's Story."

II Timothy 3:16 says "All Scripture is given by inspiration of God."

CHAPTER ONE

INTRODUCTION

Many have undertaken to draw up an account of the things that have been fulfilled among us, just as those who from the beginning were eyewitnesses and servants of the Word have handed them down to us, it seemed fitting for me (Luke) as well, having investigated everything carefully from the beginning, to write it out for you in consecutive order, so that you may know the exact truth about the things you have been taught.

In the beginning was the Word, and the Word was with God, and the Word was God. He was in the beginning with God. All things came into being through Him: and apart from Him nothing came into being that has come into being. In Him was life; and the life was the light of men. And the light shines in the darkness; and the darkness did not comprehend it. There was the true light which, coming into the world, enlightens every man. He was in the world, and the world was made through Him, and the world did not know Him. He came to His own, and those who were His own did not receive Him. But as many as received Him, to them He gave the right to become children of God, even to those who believe in His name, who were born not of blood, nor of the will of the flesh, nor of the will of man, but of God. And the Word became flesh, and dwelt among us, and we behold His glory, glory as of the only begotten from the Father, full of grace and truth.

CHAPTER TWO

In the days of Herod, king of Judea, there was a certain priest named Zacharias, of the division of Abijah; and he had a wife from the daughter of Aaron, and her name was Elizabeth. They were both righteous in the sight of God, walking blamelessly in all the commandments and requirements of the Lord. They had no child, because Elizabeth was barren, and they were both advanced in years. Now it came about, while he was perform-ing his priestly service before God in the appointed order of his division, according to the custom of the priestly office, he was chosen by lot to enter the temple of the Lord and burn incense. The whole multitude of the people were in prayer outside at the hour of the incense offering. An angel of the Lord appeared to him, standing to the right of the alter of incense. Zacharias was troubled when he saw him and fear gripped him. But the angel said to him, "Do not be afraid, Zacharias, for your petition has been heard, and your wife Elizabeth will bear you a son, and you will give him the name John. You will have joy and gladness, and many will rejoice at his birth. For he will be great in the sight of the Lord, he will drink no wine or liquor; and he will be filled with the Holy Spirit, while yet in his mother's womb. He will turn back many of the sons of Israel to the Lord their God. It is he who will go as a forerunner before Him in the spirit and power of Elijah, to turn the hearts of the fathers back to the children, and the disobedient to the attitude of the righteous; so as to make ready a people prepared for the Lord." Zacharias said to the angel, "How shall I know this for certain? For I am an old man, and my wife is advanced in years." The angel answered and said to him, "I am Gabriel, who stands in the presence of God; and I have been sent to speak to you, and to bring you this good news. Behold, you shall be silent and unable to speak until the day when these things take place, because you did not believe my words, which shall be fulfilled in their proper time." The people were waiting for Zacharias, and were wondering at his delay in the temple. But when he came out, he was unable to speak to them; and they realized that he had seen a vision in the temple; he kept making signs to them, and remained mute. It came about, when the days of his priestly service were ended, that he went back home. After these days Elizabeth his wife became pregnant; and she kept herself in seclusion for five months, saying, "This is the way the Lord has dealt with me in the days when He looked with favor upon me, to take away my disgrace among men."

Now the birth of Jesus Christ was as follows. In the sixth month the angel Gabriel was sent from God to a city in Galilee, called Nazareth, to a virgin engaged to a man whose name was Joseph, of the descendants of David; and the virgin's name was Mary. Coming in, he said to her, "Hail, favored one! The Lord is with you." But she was greatly troubled at this statement and kept pondering what kind of salutation this might be. The angel said to her, "Do not be afraid, Mary; for you have found favor with God. Behold, you will conceive in you womb, and bear a son, and you shall name Him Jesus. He will be great, and will be called the Son of the Most High; and the Lord God will give Him the throne of His father David; and He will reign over the house of Jacob forever; and His kingdom will have no end." Mary said to the angel, "How can this be, since I am a virgin?" The angel answered and said to her, "The Holy Spirit will come upon you, and power of the Most High will overshadow you; and for that reason the holy offspring shall be called the Son of God. Behold, even your relative Elizabeth has also conceived a son in her old age; and she who was called barren is now in her sixth month. For nothing will be impossible with God." Mary said, "Behold, the bondslave of the Lord; be it done to me according to your word." And the angel departed from her.

When His mother Mary had been betrothed to Joseph, before they came together she was found to be with child by the Holy Spirit.

Joseph her husband, being righteous man, and not wanting to disgrace her, desired to put her away secretly. But when he had considered this, behold, an angel of the Lord appeared to him in a dream, saying "Joseph, son of David, do not be afraid to take Mary as your wife: for that which has been conceived in her is of the Holy Spirit. She will bear a Son; and you shall call His name Jesus, for it is He who will save His people from the sins." Now all this took place that what was spoken by the Lord through the prophet might be fulfilled, saying, "Behold, the virgin shall be with child, and shall bear a son, and they shall call His name Immanuel, which translated means, "God with Us!" Joseph arose from his sleep, and did as the angel of the Lord commanded him, and took her as his wife. He kept her a virgin until she would give birth to a Son; and he would call His name Jesus.

Now at this time Mary arose and went with haste to the hill country, to a city of Judah, and entered the house of Zacharias and greeted Elizabeth. It came about that when Elizabeth heard Mary's greeting, the baby leaped in her womb; and Elizabeth was filled with the Holy Spirit. She cried out with a loud voice, and said, "Blessed among women are you, and blessed is the fruit of your womb! How has it happened to me, that the mother of my Lord should come to me? For behold, when the sound of your greeting reached my ears, the baby leaped in my womb for joy. Blessed is she who believed that there would be a fulfillment of what had been spoken to her by the Lord." And Mary said; "My soul exalts the Lord, and my spirit had rejoiced in God my Savior. For He has had regard for the humble state of His bondslave; for behold, from this time on all generations will count me blessed. For the Mighty One has done great things for me; and holy is His name. His mercy is upon generation after generation towards those who fear Him. He has done mighty deeds with His arm; He has scattered those who were proud in the thoughts of their heart. He has brought down rulers from their thrones, and has exalted those who were humble. He has filled the hungry with good things; and sent away the rich empty handed. He has given help to Israel His servant, in remembrance of His mercy, as he spoke to our fathers, to Abraham and his offspring forever." And Mary stayed with her about three months, and then returned to her home.

Now the time had come for Elizabeth to give birth, and she brought forth a son. Her neighbors and her relatives heard that the Lord had displayed his great mercy toward her, and they were rejoicing with her. It came about that on the eighth day they came to circumcise the child, and they were going to call him Zacharias, after his father. His mother answered and said, "No indeed; but he shall be called John." And they said to her, "There is no one among your relatives who is called by that name." They made signs to his father, as to what he wanted him called. He asked for a tablet, and wrote as follows, "His name is John." They were all astonished. At once his mouth was opened and his tongue loosed, and he began to speak in praise of God. Fear came on all those living around them; and all these matters were being talked about in all the hill country of Judea. All who heard them kept them in mind, saying, "What then will this child turn out to be ?" The hand of Lord was certainly with him. His father Zacharias was filled with the Holy Spirit, and prophesied, saying: "Blessed be the Lord God of Israel, for He has visited us and accomplished redemption for His people, and has raised up a horn of salvation for us in the house of David His servant as he spoke by the mouth of His holy prophets from of old—salvation from our enemies, and from the hand of all who hate us; to show mercy toward our fathers, and to remember His holy covenant, the oath which he swore to Abraham our father, to grant us that we, being delivered from the hand of our enemies, might serve Him without fear, in holiness and righteousness before Him all our days, and you, child, will be called the prophet of the Most High; for you will go on before the Lord to prepare His ways; to give to His people the knowledge of salvation by the forgiveness of their sins, because of the tender mercy of our God, with which the sunrise from on high shall visit us, to shine upon those who sit in darkness and shadow of death, to guide our feet into the way of peace." The child continued to grow, and to become strong in spirit, and he lived in the deserts until the day of his public appearance in Israel.

CHAPTER THREE

A record of the genealogy of Jesus Christ the son of David, the son of Abraham: Abraham was the father of Isaac, Isaac the father of Jacob, Jacob the father of Judah and his brothers, Judah the father of Perez and Zerah, whose mother was Tamar, Perez the father of Hezron, Hezron the father of Ram, Ram the father of Amminadab, Amminadab the father of Nahshon, Nahshon the father of Salmon, Salmon the father Boaz, whose mother was Rahab, Boaz the father of Obed, whose mother was Ruth, Obed the father of Jesse, and Jesse the father of King David. David was the father of Solomon, whose mother had been Uriah's wife, Solomon the father of Rehoboam, Rehoboam the father of Abijah, Abijah the father of Asa, Asa the father of Jehoshaphat, Jehoshaphat the father of Joram, Joram the father of Uzziah, Uzziah the father of Jotham, Jotham the father of Ahaz, Ahaz the father Hezekiah, Hezekiah the father of Manasseh, Manasseh the father of Amon, Amon the father of Josiah, and Josiah the father of Jeconiah and his brothers at the time of the exile to Babylon. After the exile to Babylon: Jeconiah was the father of Shealtiel, Shealtiel the father of Zerubbabel, Zerubbabel the father of Abiud, Abiud the father of Azor, Azor, the father of Zadok, Zadok the father of Akim, Akim the father Eliud, Eliud the father of Eleazar, Eleazar the father of Matthan, Matthan the father Jacob, and Jacob the father of **Joseph**, the husband of Mary, of whom was born Jesus, who is called Christ.

Therefore all the generations from Abraham to David are fourteen generations; and from David to the exile to Babylon fourteen generations; and from the exile to Babylon to the time of Christ fourteen generations.

Joseph is the son-in-law of Eli, (**Mary**'s family) the son of Matthat, the son of Levi, the son of Melchi, the son of Jannai, the son of Joseph, the son of Matathias, the son of Amos, the son of Naham, the son of Hesli, the son of Naggai, the son of Maath, the son of Mattathias, the son of Semein, the son of Josech, the son of Joda, the son of Joanan, the son of Rhesa, the son of Zerubbabel, the son of Shealtiel, the son of Neri, the son of Melchi, the son of Addi, the son of Cosam, the son of Elmadam, the son of Er, the son of Joshua, the son of Eliezer, the son of Jorim, the son of Matthat, the son of Levi, the son of Simeon, the son of Judah, the son of Joseph, the son of Jonam, the son of Eliakim, the son of Melea, the son of Menna, the son of Mattatha, the son of Nathan, the son of David, the son of Jesse, the son of Obed, the son of Boaz, the son of Salmon, the son of Nahshon, the son of Amminadab, the son of Admin, the son of Ram, the son of Hezron, the son of Perez, the son of Judah, the son of Jacob, the son of Isaac, the son of Abraham, the son of Terah, the son of Nahor, the son of Serug, the son of Reu, the son of Peleg, the son of Heber, the son of Shelah, the son of Cainan, the son of Arphaxad, the son of Shem, the son of Noah, the son of Lamech, the son of Methuselah, the son of Enoch, the son of Jared, the son of Mahalaleel, the son of Cainan, the son of Enosh, the son of Seth, the son of Adam, the son of God.

Chapter Four

Now it came about in those days that a decree went out from Caesar Augustus, that a census be taken of all the inhabited earth. This was the first census taken while Quirinius was governor of Syria. And all were proceeding to register for in the census, everyone to his own city. Joseph also went up from Galilee, from the city of Nazareth, to Judea, the city of David, which is called Bethlehem, because he was of the house and family of David, in order to register, along with Mary, who was engaged to him, and was with child, and it came about that while they were there, the days were completed for her to give birth. She gave birth to her first-born son; and she wrapped Him in cloths, and laid Him in a manger, because there was no room for them in the inn.

In the same region there were some shepherds staying out in the fields, and keeping watch over their flock by night. An angel of the Lord suddenly stood before them, and the glory of the Lord shone around them; and they were terribly frightened. The angel said to them, "Do not be afraid; for behold, I bring you good news of a great joy which shall be for all the people; for today in the city of David there has been born for you a Savior, who is Christ the Lord. And this will be a sign for you; you will find a baby wrapped in cloths, and lying in a manger." Suddenly there appeared with the angel a multitude of the heavenly host praising God, and saying, "Glory to God in the highest, and one earth peace among men with whom He is pleased." It came about when the angels had gone away from them into heaven, that the shepherds began saying to one another, "Let us go straight to Bethlehem then, and see this thing that has happened which the Lord has made known to us." They came in haste and found their way to Mary and Joseph, and the baby as He lay in the manger. When they had seen this, they made known the statement which had been told them about this Child. All who heard it wondered at the things which were told them by the shepherds. But Mary treasured up all these things, pondering them in her heart. The shepherds went back, glorifying and praising God for all that they had heard and seen, just as had been told them.

When eight days were completed before His circumcision, His name was then called Jesus, the name given by the angel before He was conceived in the womb. When the days for their purification according to the law of Moses were completed, they brought Him up to Jerusalem to present Him to the Lord (as it is written in the Law of the Lord, "Every first-born male that opens the womb shall be called Holy to the Lord"). And to offer a sacrifice according to what was said in the Law of the Lord, "A pair of turtledoves, or two young pigeons." Behold, there was a man in Jerusalem whose name was Simeon; and this man was righteous and devout, looking for the consolation of Israel; and the Holy Spirit was upon him. It had been revealed to him by the Holy Spirit that he would not see death before he had seen the Lord's Christ. He came in the Spirit into the temple; and when the parents brought in the child Jesus, to carry out for Him the custom of the Law, then he took Him into his arms, and blessed God, and said, "Now Lord, Thou dost let Thy bondservant depart in peace, according to Thy word; for mine eyes have seen Thy salvation, which Thou hast prepared in the presence of the peoples, a light of revelation to the gentiles, and the glory of Thy people Israel." His father and mother were amazed at the things which were being said about Him. Simeon blessed them, and said to Mary His mother, "Behold, this Child is appointed for the fall and rise of many in Israel, and for a sign to be opposed and a sword will pierce even your own soul to the end that thoughts from many hearts may be revealed." There was a prophetess, Anna the daughter of Phanuel, of the tribe of Asher. She was advanced in years, having lived with a husband seven years after her marriage, and then as a widow to the age of eighty-four. She never left the temple, serving night and day with fastings and prayers. At that very moment she came up and began giving thanks to

God, and continued to speak of Him to all those who were looking for the redemption of Jerusalem. When they had performed everything according to the Law of the Lord, they returned to Galilee, to their own city of Nazareth.

Now after Jesus was born in Bethlehem of Judea in the days of Herod the king, behold, magi from the east arrived in Jerusalem, saying, "Where is He who has been born King of the Jews? For we saw His star in the east, and have come to worship Him." And when Herod the king heard it, he was troubled, and all Jerusalem with him. Gathering together all the chief priests and scribes of the people, he began to inquire of them where the Christ was to be born. They said to him, "In Bethlehem of Judea, for so it has been written by the prophet, "And you, Bethlehem, land of Judah, are by no means least among the leaders of Judah; for out of you shall come forth a Ruler, who will shepherd my people Israel." Then Herod secretly called the magi, and ascertained from them the time the star appeared. He sent them to Bethlehem and said, "Go and make careful search for the Child; and when you have found Him, report to me, that I too may come and worship Him." Having heard the king, they went their way; and lo, the star, which they had seen in the east, went on before them, until it came and stood over where the Child was. When they saw the star, they rejoiced exceedingly with great joy. They came into the house and saw the Child with Mary His mother; and they fell down and worshiped Him; and opening their treasures, they presented to Him gifts of gold and frankincense and myrrh. Having been warned by God in a dream not to return to Herod, they departed for their own country by another way. Now when they had departed, behold, an angel of the Lord appeared to Joseph in a dream, saying, "Arise and take the Child and His mother and flee to Egypt, and remain there until I tell you; for Herod is going to search for the Child to destroy Him." He arose and took the Child and His mother by night, and departed for Egypt; and was there until the death Herod, that what was spoken by the Lord through the prophet might be fulfilled saying "Out of Egypt did I call My son." Then when Herod saw that he had been tricked by the magi, he became very enraged, and sent and slew all the male children who were in Bethlehem and in all its environs, from two years old and under, according to time which he had ascertained from the magi. Then that which was spoken through Jeremiah the prophet was fulfilled, saying, "A voice was heard in Ramah, weeping and great mourning, Rachel weeping for her children; and she refused to be comforted, because they were no more." But when Herod was dead, behold, an angel of the Lord appeared in a dream to Joseph in Egypt, saying, "Arise and take the Child and His mother, and go into the land of Israel; for those who sought the Child's life are dead." He arose and took the Child and His mother, and came into the land of Israel. When he heard that Archelaus was reigning over Judea in place of his father Herod, he was afraid to go there. Being warned by God in a dream, he departed for the regions of Galilee, and came and resided in a city called Nazareth, that what was spoken through the prophets might be fulfilled, "He shall be called a Nazarene."

The Child continued to grow and become strong, increasing in wisdom; and the grace of God was upon Him. His parents used to go to Jerusalem every year at the Feast of the Passover, and when He became twelve, they went up there according to the custom of the Feast; and as they were returning, after spending the full number of days, the boy Jesus stayed behind in Jerusalem. His parents were unaware of it, but supposed Him to be in the caravan, and were a day's journey; when they began looking for Him among their relatives and acquaintances. When they did not find Him, they returned to Jerusalem, looking for Him. It came about that after three days they found Him in the temple, sitting in the midst of the teachers, both listening to them, and asking them questions. All who heard Him were amazed at His understanding and His answers. When they saw Him, they were astonished; and His mother said to Him, "Son, why have You treated us this way? Behold, your father and I have been anxiously looking for You." He said to them, "Why is it that you were looking for me? Did you not know that I had to be in My Father's house?" They did not understand the statement which He had made to them. He went down with them, and came to Nazareth; He continued in subjection to them; and His mother treasured all there things in her heart. Jesus kept increasing in wisdom and stature, and in favor with God and men.

CHAPTER FIVE

A s it is written in Isaiah the prophet, "Behold, I send my messenger before Your face, who will prepare Your way; the voice of one crying in the wilderness, make ready the way of the Lord, make His paths straight." There came a man, sent from God, whose name was John. He came for a witness, that he might bear witness of the light, that all might believe through him. He was not the light, but came that he might bear witness of the light.

Now in the fifteenth year of the reign of Tiberius Caesar, when Pontius Pilate was governor of Judea, and Herod was tetrarch of Galilee, and his brother Philip was tetrarch of the region of Ituraea and Trachonitis, and Lysanias was tetrarch of Abilene, in the high priesthood of Annas and Caiaphas, the word of God came to John, the son of Zacharias, in the wilderness. John the Baptist came preaching in the wilderness of Judea and to all the district around the Jordan. Preaching a baptism of repentance for forgiveness of sins: saying, "Repent, for the kingdom of heaven is at hand." John bore witness of Him, and cried out, saying, "This was He of whom I said, He who comes after me has a higher rank then I, for He existed before me. For of His fullness we have all received, and grace upon grace. For the law was given through Moses; grace and truth were realized through Jesus Christ. No man has seen God at any time; the only begotten God, who is in the bosom of the Father, He has explained Him." This is the witness of John, when the Jews sent to him priests and Levites from Jerusalem to ask him, "Who are you?" and he confessed, and did not deny, he confessed, "I am not the Christ." They asked him, "What then? Are you Elijah?" He said, "I am not." "Are you the Prophet?" He answered, "No." They said then to him, "Who are you, so that we may give an answer to those who sent us? What do you say about yourself?" He said, I am the one referred to by Isaiah the prophet, saying, "The voice of one crying in the wilderness, make ready the way of the Lord, make His paths straight! Every ravine shall be filled up, and every mountain and hill shall be brought low; and the crooked shall become straight, and the rough roads smooth; and the flesh shall see the salvation of God."

John himself had a garment of camel's hair, and a leather belt about his waist; his food was locusts and wild honey. Jerusalem was going out to him, and all Judea, and all the district around the Jordan; they were being baptized by him in the Jordan River, as they confessed their sins. When he saw many of the Pharisees and Sadducees coming for baptism, he said to them. "You brood of vipers, who warned you to flee from the wrath to come? Therefore bring forth fruits in keeping with your repentance, and do not begin to say to yourselves, 'We have Abraham for our father,' for I say to you that God is able from these stones to raise up children to Abraham. Also the axe is already laid at the root of the trees: every tree therefore that does not bear good fruit is cut down and thrown into the fire." The multitudes were questioning him, saying, "Then what shall we do?" He would answer and say to them, "Let the man who has two tunics share with him who has none; and let him who has food do likewise." Some tax-gatherers also came to be baptized, and they said to him, "Teacher, what shall we do?" He said to them, "Collect no more than what you have been ordered to." Some soldiers were questioning him, saying "And what about us, what shall we do?" He said to the, "Do not take money from anyone by force, or accuse anyone falsely, and be content with your wages." Now while the people were in a state of expectation and all were wondering in their heart about John, as to whether he might be the Christ. John answered and said to them all, "As for me, I baptize you with water; but He who is mightier than I is coming, and I am not fit to untie the thong of His sandals; He Himself will baptize you in the Holy Spirit and fire. His winnowing fork is in His hand to clean out His threshing floor, and to gather the wheat into His barn; but He will burn up the chaff with unquenchable fire." So with many other exhortations also he preached the gospel to the people.

Then Jesus arrived from Galilee at the Jordan coming to John, to be baptized by him. But John tried to prevent Him, saying, "I have need to be baptized by You, and do You come to me?" Jesus answering said to him, "Permit it at this time; for in this way it is fitting for us to fulfill all righteousness." Then he permitted Him. After being baptized, Jesus went up immediately from the water; and while he was praying, heaven was opened, and he saw the Spirit of God descending as a dove, and coming upon Him, and behold, a voice out of the heaven, saying, "This is My beloved Son, in whom I am well pleased." Immediately the Spirit impelled Him to go out into the wilderness. When He began His ministry, Jesus Himself was about thirty years of age.

CHAPTER SIX

The beginning of the gospel of Jesus Christ the Son of God. Jesus, full of the Holy Spirit, returned from the Jordan and was led about by the Spirit in the wilderness for forty days and forty nights. He ate nothing during those days. He became hungry. The tempter (devil) came and said to Him, "If You are the Son of God, command that these stones become bread." Jesus answered and said, "It is written 'Man shall not live on bread alone. But on every word that proceeds out of the mouth of God.'" The devil took Him to a very high mountain, and showed Him all the kingdoms of the world, and their glory; and the devil said to Him, "I will give You all this domain and its glory; for it has been handed over to me, and I give it to whomever I wish. Therefore if You fall down and worship me, it shall all be Yours." Jesus answered and said to him, "It is written, 'You shall worship the Lord Your God and serve Him only.'" Then the devil led Him to Jerusalem and set Him on the pinnacle of the temple, and said to Him, "If You are the Son of God, cast Yourself down from here for it is written. 'He will give His angels charge concerning You, and on their hands they will bear You up, lest You strike Your foot against a stone.'" Jesus said to him, "Begone Satan! For it is written 'You shall not force a test on the Lord your God.'" The devil left Him; and behold, angels came and minister to Him.

Jesus returned to Galilee in the power of the Spirit: and news about Him spread through all the surrounding district. He began teaching in their synagogues and was praised by all. He came to Nazareth, where He had been brought up; and as was His custom, he entered the synagogue on the Sabbath, and stood up to read. The book of the prophet Isaiah was handed to Him. He opened the book, and found the place where it was written. "The Spirit of the Lord is upon Me, because He anointed Me to preach the gospel to the poor, He has sent Me to proclaim release to the captive, and recovery of sight to the blind, to set free those who are downtrodden, to proclaim the favorable year of the Lord." He closed the book, and gave it back to the attendant, and sat down; and the eyes of all in the synagogue were fixed upon Him. He began to say to them. "Today this Scripture has been fulfilled in your hearing." All were speaking well of Him, and wondering at the gracious words which were falling from his lips; and they were saying, "Is this not Joseph's son?" He said to them, "No doubt you will quote this proverb to Me, 'Physician, heal yourself; whatever we heard was done at Capernaum, do here in your home town as well.'" He said, "Truly I say to you, no prophet is welcome in his home town. But I say to you in truth, there were many widows in Israel in the days of Elijah, when the sky was shut up for three years and six months, when a great famine came over all the land; and yet Elijah was sent to none of them, but only to Zarephath, in the land of Sidon, to a woman who was a widow. There were many lepers in Israel in the time of Elisha the prophet; and none of them was cleansed, but only Naaman the Syrian." All the Synagogue were filled with rage as they heard these things; and they rose up and cast Him out of the city, and led Him to the brow of the hill on which their city had been built, in order to throw Him down the cliff. **But passing through their midst, He went His way.**

He came down to Capernaum, a city of Galilee. He was teaching them on the Sabbath day; and they were continually amazed at His teaching, for his message was with authority. There was a man in the synagogue possessed by the spirit of an unclean demon, and he cried out with a loud voice, "Ha! What do we have to do with You, Jesus of Nazareth? Have You come to destroy us? I know who You are – the Holy One of God!" Jesus rebuked him, saying, "Be quiet and come out of him!" When the demon had thrown him down in their midst, he went out of him without doing him any harm. Amazement came upon them all, and they began discussing with one another, and saying, "What is this message? For with authority and power He commands the unclean spirits, and they come out."

The report about Him was getting out into every locality in the surrounding district. It came about that while the multitude were pressing around Him and listening to the word of God, Jesus was walking along the Sea of Galilee, which is the region of Zebulin and Naphtali, he was preaching the gospel of God. He was saying, "The time is fulfilled and the kingdom of God is at hand, repent and believe in the gospel." This is to fulfill what was spoken through Isaiah the prophet, saying, "The land of Zebulun and the land of Naphtali, by the way of the sea, beyond the Jordan, Galilee of the gentiles, the people who were sitting in darkness saw a great light, and to those who were sitting in the land and shadow of death, upon them a light dawned."

John bore witness saying, "I have beheld the Spirit descending as dove out of heaven; and He remained upon Him. He who sent me to baptize in water said to me, 'He upon whom you see the Spirit descending and remaining upon Him, this is the one who baptized in the Holy Spirit.' I have seen, have borne witness that this is the Son of God. Behold, the Lamb of God who takes away the sin of the world! This is He on behalf of whom I said, 'After me comes a Man who has a higher rank than I, for He existed before me.'" John was with two of his disciples; when he looked upon Jesus as He walked, and said, "Behold, the Lamb of God!"

Jesus saw two boats lying at the edge of the lake; but the fishermen had gotten out of them, and was washing their nets. He got into one of the boats, which was Simon's, and asked him to put out a little way from the land. He sat down and began teaching the multitudes from the boat. When He had finished speaking, He said to Simon, "Put out into the deep water and let down your nets for a catch." Simon answered and said, "Master, we worked hard all night and caught nothing, but at Your bidding I will let down the nets." When they had done this, they enclosed a great quantity of fish; and their nets began to break; they signaled to their partners in the other boat, for them to come and help them. They came, and filled both of the boats, so that they began to sink.

When Simon saw that, he fell down at Jesus' feet, saying, "Depart from me, for I am a sinful man, O Lord!" For amazement had seized him and all his companions because of the catch of fish which they had taken. Jesus looked at him, and said, "You are Simon the son of John, you shall be called Peter." Simon's brother Andrew said, "We have found the Messiah." The two disciples followed Jesus. As He was walking He saw James the son of Zebedee, and John his brother in their boats mending their nets. Immediately He called them; "Follow Me, and I will make you fishers of men." They left their father Zebedee in the boat with the hired servants, and went away to follow Him. The next day he purposed to go forth into Galilee, and He found Philip, and Jesus said to him, "Follow me." Now Philip was from Bethsaida, of the city of Andrew and Peter. Philip found Nathanael, and said to him, "We have found Him of whom Moses in the Law and also the Prophets wrote, Jesus of Nazareth, the son of Joseph." Nathanael said to him, "Can any good thing come out of Nazareth?" Philip said to him, "Come and see." Jesus saw Nathanael coming to Him, and said of him, "Behold an Israelite indeed, in whom is no guile!" Nathanael said to Him, "How do You know me?" Jesus answered and said to him, "Before Philip called you, when you were under the fig tree, I saw you." Nathanael answered Him "Rabbi, You are the Son of God; You are the King of Israel." Jesus answered and said to him "Because I said to you that I saw you under the fig tree, do you believe? You shall see greater things than these." He said to him, "Truly, truly, I say you shall see the heavens opened, and the angels of God ascending and descending upon the Son of Man."

CHAPTER SEVEN

There was a wedding in Cana of Galilee; the mother of Jesus was there; and Jesus also was invited, and His disciples, to the wedding. When the wine gave out, the mother of Jesus said to Him, "They have no wine." Jesus said to her, "Woman, what do I have to do with you? My hour has not yet come." His mother said to the servants, "Whatever He says to you, do it." Now there were six stone waterpots set there for the Jewish custom of purification, containing twenty or thirty gallons each. Jesus said to them, "Fill the waterpots with water." They filled them up to the brim. He said to them, "Draw some out now, and take it to the headwaiter." They took it to him. When the headwaiter tasted the water which had become wine, and did not know where it came from (but the servants who had drawn the water knew), the headwaiter called the bridegroom, and said to him, "Every man serves the good wine first, and when men have drunk freely, then that which is poorer; you have kept the good wine until now." This beginning of His signs Jesus did in Cana of Galilee, and manifested His glory, and His disciples believed in Him.

After this He went down to Capernaum, He and His mother, and His brothers, and His disciples; there they stayed a few days. The Passover of Jews was at hand, and Jesus went up to Jerusalem. He found in the temple those who were selling oxen and sheep and doves, and moneychangers seated. He made a scourge of cords, and drove them all out of the temple, with the sheep and the oxen; and He poured out the coins of the moneychanger, and overturned their tables; and to those who were selling the doves He said, "Take these things away;

stop making My Father's house a house of merchandise." His disciples remembered that it was written, "Zeal for the house will consume me." The Jews therefore answered and said to Him, "What sign do You show to us, seeing that You do these things?" Jesus answered and said to them, "Destroy this temple, and in three days I will raise it up." The Jews said, "It took fortysix years to build this temple, and will You raise it up in three days?' But He was speaking of the temple of His body. Now when He was in Jerusalem at the Passover, during the feast, many believed in His name, beholding His signs which He was doing. But Jesus, on His part, was not entrusting Himself to them, for He knew all men, and because He did not need any one to bear witness concerning man for He Himself knew what was in man.

Chapter Eight

Now there was a man of the Pharisees, named Nicodemus, a ruler of the Jews, this man came to Him by night, and said to Him, "Rabbi, we know that You have come from God as a teacher; for no one can do these signs that You do unless God is with him." Jesus answered and said to him, "Truly, truly, I say to you, unless one is born again, he cannot see the kingdom of God." Nicodemus said to Him, "How can a man be born when he is old? He cannot enter a second time into his mother's womb and be born, can he?" Jesus answered, "Truly, truly, I say to you, unless one is born of water and the Spirit, he cannot enter unto the kingdom of God. That which is born of the flesh is flesh; and that which is born of the Spirit is Spirit. Do not marvel that I said to you, 'You must be born again.' The wind blows where it wishes and you hear the sound of it, but do not know where it comes from and where it is going; so is every one who is born of the Spirit." Nicodemus answered and said to Him, "How can these things be?" Jesus answered and said to him, "Are you the teacher of Israel, and do not understand these things? Truly, truly, I say to you, we speak that which we know, and bear witness of that which we have seen; and you do not receive our witness. If I told you earthly things and you do not believe, how shall you believe if I tell you heavenly things? And no one has ascended into heaven, but He who descended from heaven, even the Son of Man. As Moses lifted up the serpent in the wilderness, even so must the Son of Man be lifted up; that whoever believes may in Him have eternal life. For God so loved the world, that He gave His only begotten Son, that whoever believes in Him should not perish, but have eternal life. For

God did not send the Son into the world to judge the world; but that the world should be saved through Him. He who believes in Him is not judged; he who does not believe has been judged already, because he has not believed in the name of the only begotten Son of God. And this in the judgment, that the light is come into the world, and men loved the darkness rather than light; for their deeds were evil. For everyone who does evil hates the light, and does not come to the light, lest his deeds should be exposed. But he who practices the truth comes to the light, that his deeds may be manifested as having been wrought in God."

After these thing Jesus and His disciples came into the land of Judea; and there He was spending time with them, and baptizing. John also was baptizing in Aenon near Salim, because there was much water there; and they were coming, and were being baptized. There arose a discussion on the part of John's disciples with a Jew about purification. They came to John, and said to him, "Rabbi, He who was with you beyond the Jordan, to whom you have borne witness, behold, he is baptizing, and all are coming to Him." John answered and said, "A man can receive nothing unless it has been given him from heaven. You yourselves bear me witness, that I said, 'I am not the Christ', but, 'I have been sent before Him.' He who has the bride is the bridegroom; but the friend of the bridegroom, who stand and bears him, rejoices greatly because of the bridegroom's voice. So this joy of mine has been made full. He must increase, but I must decrease. He who comes from above is above all, he who is of the earth is from the earth and speaks of the earth. He who comes from heaven is above all. What He has seen and heard, of that He bears witness; and no man receives His witness. He who has received His witness has set his seal to this, that God is true. For He whom God has sent speaks the words of God; for He gives the Spirit without measure. The Father loves the Son, and has givin all things into His hand. He who believes the Son has eternal life; but he who does not obey the Son shall not see life, but the wrath of God abides on him." When therefore the Lord knew that the Pharisees had heard that He was making and baptizing more disciples than John (although Jesus Himself was not baptizing, but His disciples were), He left Judea, and departed again into Galilee.

CHAPTER NINE

He came to a city of Samaria, called Sychar, near the parcel of ground that Jacob gave to his son Joseph; and Jacob's well was there. Jesus, being wearied from His journey, was sitting thus by the well. It was about the sixth hour. There came a woman of Samaria to draw water. Jesus said to her, "Give Me a drink." For His disciples had gone away into the city to buy food. The Samaritan woman said to Him, "How is it that You, being a Jew, ask me for a drink since I am a Samaritan woman?" (For Jews have no dealings with Samaritans.) Jesus answered and said to her, "If you knew the gift of God, and who it is who says to you, 'Give Me a drink.' You would have asked Him, and He would have given you living water." She said to Him, "Sir, You have nothing to draw with and the well is deep; where then do You get that living water? You are not greater than our father Jacob, are You, who gave us the well, and drank of it himself, and his sons, and his cattle?" Jesus answered and said to her, "Everyone who drinks of this water shall thirst again; but whoever drinks of the water that I shall give him shall never thirst; but the water that I shall give him shall become in him a well of water springing up to eternal life." The woman said to Him, "Sir, give me this water, so I will not be thirsty, nor come all the way here to draw." He said to her, "Go, call your husband, and come here," The woman answered and said, "I have no husband." Jesus said to her, "You have well said, 'I have no husband'; for you have had five husbands; and the one whom you now have is not your husband; this you have said truly." The woman said to Him, "Sir, I perceive that You are a prophet. Our fathers worshiped in this mountain; and you people say that in Jerusalem is the place where men ought to worship." Jesus said to her, "Woman, believe Me, an hour is coming when neither in this mountain, nor in Jerusalem, shall you worship the Father. You worship that which you do not know; we worship that which we know; for salvation is from the Jews. But an hour is coming, and now is, when the true worshipers shall worship the Father in spirit and truth; for such people the Father seeks to be His worshipers. God is Spirit; and those who worship Him must worship in spirit and truth." The woman said to Him, "I know the Messiah is coming (He who is called Christ); when that One comes, He will declare all things to us." Jesus said to her, "I who speak to you am He."

At this point His disciples came, and they marveled that He had been speaking with a woman; yet no one said, "What do You seek?" or "Why do You speak with her?" So the woman left her waterpot, and went into the city, and said to the men, "Come, see a man who told me all the things that I have done; this is not the Christ, is it?" They went out of the city, and were coming to Him. In the meanwhile the disciples were requesting Him, saying, "Rabbi eat." But He said to them, "I have food to eat that you do not know about." The disciples therefore were saying to one another, "No one brought Him anything to eat, did he?" Jesus said to them, "My food is to do the will of Him who sent Me, and to accomplish His work. Do you not say, 'There are yet four months, and then come the harvest?' Behold, I say to you, lift up your eyes, and look on the fields, that they are white for harvest. Already he who reaps is receiving wages, and is gathering fruit for life eternal; that he who sows and he who reaps may rejoice together. For in this case the saying is true, 'One sows, and another reaps.' I sent you to reap that for which you have not labored; others have labored, and you have entered into their labor." From that city many of the Samaritans believed in Him because of the word of the woman who testified, "He told me all the things that I have done." So when the Samaritans came to Him, they were asking Him to stay with them; and He stayed there two days. Many more believed because of His word; and they were saying to the woman, "It is no longer because of what you said that we believe, for we have heard for ourselves and know that this One is indeed the Savior of the world."

After the two days He went forth from there into Galilee. For Jesus Himself testified that a prophet has not honor in his own country. So when He came to Galilee, the Galileans received Him, having seen all the things that He did in Jerusalem at the feast; for they themselves also went to the feast. He came again to Cana of Galilee where He had made the water wine. There was a certain royal official, whose son was sick at Capernaum. When he heard that Jesus had come out of Judea into Galilee, he went to Him, and was requesting Him to come down and heal his son; for he was at the point of death. Jesus said to him, "Unless you people see signs and wonders, you simply will not believe." The royal official said to Him, "Sir, come down before my child dies." Jesus said to him, "Go your way; your son lives." The man believed the word of Jesus spoke to him, and he started off. As he was now going down, his slaves met him, saying that his son was living. So he inquired of them the hour when he began to get better. They said to him, "Yesterday at the seventh hour the fever left him." The father knew that it was at that hour in which Jesus said to him, "Your son lives"; and he himself believed, and his whole household.

CHAPTER TEN

Herod the tetrarch was reproved by John the Baptist. Herod himself had sent and had John arrested and bound in prison on account of Herodias, the wife of his brother Philip, because he had married her. For John had been saying to Herod, "It is not lawful for you to have your brother's wife." And Herodias had a grudge against him and wanted to kill him; and could not do so; for Herod was afraid of John, knowing that he was a righteous and holy man. He kept him safe. When Herod heard John, he was very perplexed; but he used to enjoy listening to him.

Now when Jesus heard that John had been taken into custody, He withdrew into Galilee, preaching the gospel of God. When Jesus returned to Galilee in the power of the Spirit; news about him spread through all the surrounding district. Jesus was going about teaching in their synagogues and was praised by all. He was proclaiming the gospel of the kingdom, and healing every kind of disease and every kind of sickness among the people. The news about Him went out into all Syria; and they brought to Him all who were ill, taken with various diseases and pain, demoniacs, epileptics, paralytics; and He healed them. Great multitudes followed Him from Galilee and Decapolis and Jerusalem and Judea and from beyond the Jordan.

CHAPTER ELEVEN

Jesus arose and left the synagogue, with Simon, Andrew, James and John, and entered Simon's (Peter) home. Now Simon's mother-in-law was suffering from a high fever; and they made request of Him on her behalf. Standing over her, He rebuked the fever, He took her by the hand, raised her up and left her; and she immediately arose and began to wait on them. While the sun was setting, all who had any sickness with various diseases brought them to Him; and laying His hands on every one of them, He was healing them. The whole city had gathered at the door. Demons also were coming out of many, crying out and saying, "You are the Son of God!" Rebuking them, He would not allow them to speak, because they knew Him to be the Christ.

When day came, He departed and went to a lonely place; and was praying there, and the multitudes were searching for Him, and came to Him, and tried to keep Him from going away from them. But He said to them, "I must preach the kingdom of God to the other cities also, for I was sent for this purpose." And He kept on preaching in the synagogues of Judea. He was preaching and casting out demons. It came about that while He was in one of the cities, behold, there was a man full of leprosy; and when he saw Jesus, he fell on his face and implored Him, saying, "Lord, if You are willing, You can make me clean." He was moved with compassion. He stretched out His hand, and touched him, saying, "I am willing; be cleansed." Immediately the leprosy left him. He ordered him to tell no one, "But go and show yourself to the priest, and make an offering for your cleansing, just as Moses commanded, for a testimony to them." He went out and began to proclaim it freely and to spread the news about, to such an extent that Jesus could no longer publicly enter a city, but stayed out in unpopulated areas. News about Him was spreading even farther, and great multitudes were gathering to hear Him and be healed of their sicknesses.

He Himself would often slip away to the wilderness and pray. When He had come back to Capernaum several days afterward, it was heard that He was at home. Many were gathered together, so that there was no longer room, even near the door; and He was speaking the word to them. Some Pharisees and teachers of the law sitting there, who had come from every village of Galilee and Judea and from Jerusalem, and the power of the Lord was present for Him to perform healing. Behold, some men were carrying on a bed a man who was paralyzed, and they were trying to bring him in, and to set him down in front of Him. Not finding any way to bring him in because of the crowd, they went up on the roof and let him down through the tiles with his stretcher, right in the center, in front of Jesus. Seeing their faith, He said, "Friend, your sins are forgiven you." The scribes and the Pharisees began to reason, saying, "Who is this man who speaks blasphemies? Who can forgive sins, but God alone?" Jesus, perceiving in His spirit that they were reasoning that way within themselves, answered and said to them, "Why are you reasoning in your hearts? Which is easier, to say, 'Your sins have been forgiven you,' or say, 'Rise and walk?' But in order that you may know that the Son of Man has authority on earth to forgive sin." He said to the paralytic, "I say to you, rise, and take up the stretcher and go home." At once he rose up before them, and took up what he had been lying on, and went home, glorifying God. They were all seized with astonishment and began glorifying God; and they were filled with fear, saying, "We have seen remarkable things today."

CHAPTER TWELVE

Jesus then went out again by the seashore; and all the multitude were coming to Him, and He was teaching them. And as He passed by, He noticed a tax-gatherer named Levi (Matthew), sitting in the tax office, and He said to him, "Follow Me." He left everything behind, and rose up and began to follow Him. Levi gave a big reception for Him in his house; and there was a great crowd of tax-gatherers and other people who were reclining at table with them. The Pharisees and scribes began grumbling at His disciples, saying, "Why do you eat and drink with the tax-gatherers and sinners?" Jesus answered and said to them, "It is not those who are well who need a physician, but those who are sick. I have not come to call righteous men but sinners to repentance." They said to Him, "The disciples of John often fast and offer prayers; the disciples of the Pharisees also do the same, but Yours eat and drink." Jesus said to them, "You cannot make the attendants of the bridegroom fast while the bridegroom is with them, can you? But the days will come; and when the bridegroom is taken away from them, then they will fast in those days." He was also telling them a parable: "No one tears a piece from a new garment and puts it on an old garment; otherwise he will tear both, and the piece from the new will not match the old. And no one puts new wine into old wineskins; otherwise the new wine will bust the skins, and it will be spilled out, and the skins will be ruined. But new wine must be put into fresh wineskins. And no one, after drinking old wine wishes for new; for he says, 'The old is good enough.'"

After these things was a feast of the Jews: and Jesus went up to Jerusalem. Now there is in Jerusalem by the sheep gate a pool, which is called in Hebrew Bethesda, having five porticoes. In these lay a multitude of those who were sick, blind, lame, and withered. (Waiting for the moving of the waters; for an angel of the Lord went down at certain seasons into the pool, and stirred up the water; whoever then first, after the stirring up of the water, stepped in was made well from whatever disease with which he was afflicted.) A certain man was there, who had been thirty-eight years in his sickness. When Jesus saw him lying there, and knew that he had already been a long time in that condition. He said to him, "Do you wish to get well?" The sick man answered Him, "Sir, I have no man to put me into the pool when the water is stirred up, but while I am coming, another steps down before me." Jesus said to him, "Arise, take up your pallet, and walk." Immediately the man became well, and took up his pallet and began to walk. Now it was the Sabbath on that day. Therefore the Jews were saying to him who was cured. "It is the Sabbath, and it is not permissible for you to carry your pallet." He answered them, "He who made me well was the one who said to me, 'Take up your pallet and walk.'" They asked him, "Who is the man who said to you, "Take up your pallet, and walk?" He who was healed did not know who it was; for Jesus had slipped away while there was a crowd in that place. Afterward Jesus found him in the temple, and said to him, "Behold, you have become well, do no sin any more, so that nothing worse may befall you." The man went away, and told the Jews that it was Jesus who had made him well.

And for this reason the Jews were persecuting Jesus, because He was doing these things on the Sabbath. He answered them, "My Father is working until now, and I Myself am working." For this cause the Jews were seeking all the more to kill Him, because He not only was breaking the Sabbath, but also was calling God His own Father, making Himself equal with God. Jesus therefore answered and was saying to them, "Truly, truly, I say to you, the Son can do nothing of Himself, unless it is something He sees the Father doing; for whatever the Father does, these things the Son also does in like manner. For the Father loves the Son, and shows Him all things that He Himself is doing; and greater works than these will He show Him, that you may marvel. For just as the Father raises the dead and gives them life, even so the Son also gives life to whom He wishes. For not even the Father judges any one, but He has given all judgment to the Son, in order that all may honor the Son, even as they honor the Father. He who does not honor the Son does not honor the Father who sent Him. Truly, truly, I say to you, he who hears My word, and believes Him who sent Me, has eternal life, and does not come into judgment, but has passed out of death into life. Truly, truly, I say to you, an hour is coming and now is, when the dead shall hear the voice of the Son of God; and those who hear shall live. For just as the Father has life in Himself, even so He gave to the Son also to have life in Himself; and He gave Him authority to execute judgment, because He is the Son of Man. Do not marvel at this; for an hour is coming, in which all who are in the tombs shall hear His voice, and shall come forth; those who did the good deeds, to a resurrection of life, those who committed the evil deeds to a resurrection of judgment. I can do nothing on My own initiative. As I hear, I judge; and My judgment is just, because I do not seek My own will, but the will of Him who sent Me.

If I alone bear witness of Myself, My testimony is not true. There is another who bears witness of Me; and I know that the testimony which He bears of Me is true. You have sent of John, and He has borne witness to the truth. But the witness which I receive is not from man: but I say these things, that you may be saved. He was the lamp that was burning and was shining and you were willing to rejoice for a while in his light. But the witness which I have is greater than of John; for the works which the Father has given Me to accomplish, the very works that I do, bear witness of Me, that the Father has sent Me. And the Father who sent Me, He has borne witness of Me. You have neither heard His voice at any time, nor seen His form. And you do not have His word abiding in you, for you do not believe Him whom He sent. You search the Scriptures, because you think that in them you have eternal life; and it is these that bear witness of Me; and you are unwilling to come to Me, that you may have life. I do no receive glory from men; But I know you, that you do not have the love of God in yourselves. I have come in My Father's name, and you do not receive Me; if another shall come in his own name, you will receive him. How can you believe, when you receive glory from one another, and you do not seek the glory that is from the one and only God? Do not think that I will accuse you before the Father; the one who accuse you is Moses, in whom you have set your hope. For if you believed Moses, you would believe Me; for he wrote of Me. But if you do not believe his writings, how will you believe My words?"

Now it came about that on a certain Sabbath he was passing through some grainfields; and His disciples were picking and eating the heads of wheat, rubbing them in their hands. But some of the Pharisees said, "Why do you do what is not lawful on the Sabbath?" Jesus answering them said, "Have you not even read what David did when he was hungry, he and those who were with him, when he entered the house of God, and took and ate the consecrated bread which is not lawful for any to eat except the priests alone, and gave it to his companions? Or have you not read in the Law, that on the Sabbath the priests in the temple break the Sabbath, and are innocent? But I say to you, that something greater than the temple is here. But if you had known what this means, 'I desire compassion, and not a sacrifice,' you would not have condemned the innocent." He was saying to them, "The Son of Man is Lord of the Sabbath." It came about on another Sabbath, that He entered the synagogue and was teaching; and there was a man there whose right hand was withered. The scribes and the Pharisees were watching Him closely, to see if He healed on the Sabbath, in order that they might find reason to accuse Him. He knew they were thinking, and He said to the man with the withered hand, "Arise and come forward!" he arose and came forward. Jesus said to them, "What man shall there be among you, who shall have one sheep, and if it falls into a pit on the Sabbath, will he no take hold of it, and lift it out? Of how much more value then is a man than a sheep! I ask you, is it lawful on the Sabbath to do good, or to do evil, to save a life, or to destroy it?" After looking around at them all, He said to him, "Stretch out you hand!" He did so; and his hand was completely restored. The Pharisees went out and immediately began taking counsel with the Herodians against Him, as to how they might destroy Him. Jesus aware of this, withdrew from there. Many followed Him, and He healed them all, and warned them not to make Him known, in order that what was spoken through Isaiah the prophet, might be fulfilled, saying "Behold, My servant whom I have chosen; My beloved in whom My soul is well-pleased; I will put my Spirit upon Him, and He shall proclaim justice to the gentiles. He will not quarrel, nor cry out; nor will any one hear His voice in the streets. A battered reed He will not break off, and smoldered wick He will not put out, until He leads justice to victory, and in His name the gentiles will have hope." It was at this time that He went off to the mountain to pray, and He spent the whole night in prayer to God.

When day came, He called His disciples to Him; and chose twelve of them, whom He also named as apostles; Simon, whom He also named Peter, and Andrew his brother; James and John the sons of Zebedee (to them He gave the name Boanerges, which means, Sons of Thunder); Philip and Bartholomew; Matthew and Thomas; James the son of Alphaeus, and Simon who was called the Zealot (the Cananaean); Judas the son of James (Thaddaeus), and Judas Iscaroit, who became a traitor. He appointed them that they might be with Him, and that He might send them out to preach, and to have authority to cast out the demons. They would heal every kind of disease and every kind of sickness. He descended with them, and stood on a level place; and a great multitude from Galilee followed; and also from Judea, and from Jerusalem, and from Idumea, and beyond the Jordan, and the vicinity of Tyre and Sidon, a great multitude heard of all that He was doing and came to Him.

CHAPTER THIRTEEN

Jesus saw the multitudes, He sat down, His disciples came to Him. Opening His mouth He began to teach them, saying "Blessed are the poor in spirit, for theirs is the kingdom of heaven. Blessed are those who mourn, for they shall be comforted. Blessed are those who are gentle, for they shall inherit the earth. Blessed are those who hunger and thirst for righteousness, for they shall be satisfied. Blessed are the merciful, for they shall receive Mercy. Blessed are the pure in heart, for they shall see God. Blessed are you who weep now, for you shall laugh. Blessed are the peacemaker, for they shall be called sons of God. Blessed are those who have been persecuted for the sake of righteousness, for theirs is the kingdom of heaven. Blessed are you when men revile you, and persecute you, and say all kinds evil against you falsely, on account of Me. Rejoice, and be glad, for your reward in heaven is great, for so they persecuted the prophets who were before you. You are the salt of the earth; but if the salt has become tasteless, how will it be made salty again? It is good for nothing any more, except to be thrown out and trampled under foot by men. You are the light of the world. A city set on a hill cannot be hidden. Nor do men light a lamp, and put it under the peck-measure, but on the lampstand; and it gives light to all who are in the house. Let your light shine before men in such a way that they may see your good works, and glorify your Father who is in heaven.

Woe to you who are rich, for you are receiving your comfort in full. Woe to you who are well-fed now, for you shall be hungry. Woe to you who laugh now, for you shall mourn and weep. Woe to you when all men speak well of you, for in the same way their fathers used to treat the false prophets.

But I say to you who hear, love your enemies, do good to those who hate you, bless those who curse you, pray for those who mistreat you. Do not think that I came to abolish the Law or the Prophets; I did not come to abolish, but to fulfill. For truly I say to you, until heaven and earth pass away, not the smallest letter or stroke shall pass away from the Law, until all is accomplished. Whoever then annuls one of the least of these commandments, and so teaches others, shall be called least in the kingdom of heaven; but whoever keeps and teaches them, he shall be called great in the kingdom of heaven. For I say to you, that unless your righteousness surpasses that of the scribes and Pharisees, you shall not enter the kingdom of heaven. You have heard the ancients were told, 'You shall not commit murder' and 'Whoever commits murder shall be liable to the court.' But I say to you that every one who is angry with his brother shall be guilty before the court; and whoever shall say to his brother, 'Raca'(good for nothing) shall be guilty before the supreme court; and whoever shall say, 'You fool' shall be guilty enough to go into the hell of fire. If therefore you are presenting your offering at the altar, and there remember that your brother has something against you, leave your offering there before the altar, and go your way; first be reconciled to your brother, and then come and present your offering. Make friends quickly with your opponent at law while you are with him on the way, in order that your opponent may not deliver you to the judge, and the judge to the officer, and you be thrown into prison. Truly I say to you, you shall not come out of there, until you have paid up the last cent. You have heard that it was said, 'You shall not commit adultery'; but I say to you, that one who looks on a woman to lust for her has committed adultery with her already in his heart. And if your right eye makes you stumble, tear it out, and throw it from you; for it is better for you that one of the parts of your body perish, than for your whole body to be thrown in hell. And if your right hand makes you stumble, cut it off, and throw it from you; for it is better for you that one of the parts of your body perish, than for your whole body to go into hell. Where their worm does not die; and the fire is not quenched. And it was said,

'Whoever divorces his wife, let him give her a certificate of dismissal'; but I say to you that every one who divorces his wife, except for the cause of unchastity, makes her commit adultery, and whoever marries a divorced woman commits adultery. Again, you have heard that the ancients were told, 'You shall not make false vows, but shall fulfill your vows to the Lord.' But I say to you, make no oath at all, either by heaven, for it is the throne of God, or by the earth, for it is the footstool of His feet, or by Jerusalem, for it is the city of the great King. Nor shall you make an oath by your ear, for you cannot make one hair white or black. But let you statement be, 'Yes, yes' or 'No, no'; and anything beyond these is of evil.

You have heard that it was said, 'An eye for and eye, and tooth for a tooth.' But I say to you, do not resist him who is evil; but whoever slaps you on your right cheek, turn to him the other also. And if one wants to sue you, and take your shirt, let him have your coat also. And whoever shall force you to go one mile, go with him two. Give to him who asks of you, and do not turn away from him who wants to borrow from you. You have heard that it was said, 'You shall love your neighbor, and hate your enemy.' But I say to you, love your enemies, and pray for those who persecute you in order that you may be sons of your Father who is in heaven; for He causes His sun to rise on the evil and the good, and sends rain on the righteous and the unrighteous. For if you love those who love you, what reward have you? Do not even the tax-gatherers do the same? And if you greet your brothers only, what do you do more than others? Do not even the Gentiles do the same? Therefore you are to be perfect, as your heavenly Father is perfect. Beware of practicing your righteousness before men to be noticed by them; otherwise you have no reward with your Father who is in heaven. When you give alms, do not sound a trumpet before you, as the hypocrites do in the synagogues and in the streets, that they may be honored by men. Truly I say to you, they have their reward in full. But when you give alms, do not let your left hand know what your right hand is doing that your alms may be in secret; and your Father who sees in secret will repay you. And when you pray, you are not to be as the hypocrites; for they love to stand and pray in the synagogues and on the street corners, in order to be seen by men. Truly I say to you, they have their reward in full. But you, when you pray, go into your inner room, and when you have shut your door, pray to your Father who is in secret, and your Father who sees in secret will repay you. And when you are praying, do not use meaningless repetition, as the Gentiles do, for they suppose that they will be heard for their many words. Therefore do not be like them; for your Father knows what you need, before you ask Him. And if you forgive men for their transgressions, your heavenly Father will also forgive you. But if you do not forgive men, then your Father will not forgive your transgressions. And whenever you fast, do not put on a gloomy face as the hypocrites do, for they neglect their appearance in order to be seen fasting by men. Truly I say to you, they have their reward in full. But you, when you fast, anoint your head, and wash your face so that you may not be seen fasting by men, but by your Father who is in secret; and your Father who sees in secret will repay you. Do not lay up for yourselves treasures upon earth, where moth and rust destroy, and where thieves break in and steal. But lay up for yourselves treasures in heaven, where neither moth nor rust destroys, and where thieves do not break in or steal; for where your treasure is, there will your heart be also. The lamp of the body is the eye; if your eye is clear, your whole body will be full of light. But if your eye is bad, your whole body will be full of darkness. If the light that is in you is darkness, how great is the darkness! No one can serve two masters; for either hate the one and love the other, or he will hold to one and despise the other, you cannot serve God and mammon (riches).

For this reason I say to you, do not be anxious for your life; as to what you shall eat, or what you shall drink; nor for your body, as to what you shall put on. Is not life more than food, and the body than clothing? Look at the birds of the air, that they do not sow, neither do they reap, nor gather into barns, and yet your heavenly Father feeds them. Are you not worth much more than they? And which of you by being anxious can add a single cubit to his life's span? And why are you anxious about clothing? Observe how the lilies of the field grow; they do not toil nor do they spin, yet I say to you that even Solomon in all his glory did not cloth himself like one of these. But if God so arrays the grass of the field, which is alive today and tomorrow is thrown into the furnace, will He not much more do so for you, O men of little faith? Do not be anxious then, saying, 'What shall we eat?' or 'What shall we drink?' or 'With what shall we cloth ourselves?' for all these things the Gentiles eagerly seek; for your heavenly Father knows that you need all these things. But seek first His Kingdom and His righteousness; and all these things shall be added to you. Therefore do not be anxious for tomorrow; for tomorrow will care for itself. Each day has enough trouble of its own.

Do not judge lest you be judged yourselves. For in the way you judge, you will be judged; and by your standard of measure, it shall be measured to you." And He also spoke a parable to them; "A blind man cannot guide a blind man, can he? Will they not both fall into a pit? A pupil is not above his teacher; but everyone, after he has been fully trained, will be like his teacher. And why do you look at the speck in your brother's eye, but do not notice the log that is in your own eye? Or how can you say to your brother, 'Let me take the speck out of your eye,' and behold, the log is in you own eye? You hypocrite, first take the log out of your eye, and then you will see clearly enough to take the speck out of your brother's eye.

Give, and it will be given to you; good measure, pressed down, shaken together, running over, they will pour into your lap. For whatever measure you deal out to others, it will be dealt to you in return. Do not give what is holy to dogs, and do not throw your pearls before swine, lest they trample them under their feet, and turn and tear you to pieces. Ask, and it shall be given to you; seek, and you shall find; knock, and it shall be opened to you. For everyone who asks receives, and he who seeks finds, and to him who knocks it shall be opened. Or what man is there among you, when his son shall ask him for a loaf, will give him a stone? Or if he shall ask for a fish, he will not give him a snake, will he? If you then, being evil, know how to give good gifts to your children, how much more shall your Father who is in heaven give what is good to those who ask Him! Therefore whatever you want others to do for you, do so for them, for this is the Law and the Prophets.

Enter by the narrow gate; for the gate is wide, and the way is broad that leads to destruction, and many are those who enter by it. For the gate is small, and the way is narrow that leads to life, and few are those who find it. Beware of the false prophets, who come to you in sheep's clothing, but inwardly are ravenous wolves. You will know them by their fruits. Grapes are not gathered from thorn bushes, nor figs from thistles, are they? Even so, every good tree bears good fruit; but the rotten tree bears bad fruit. A good tree cannot produce bad fruit, nor can a rotten tree produce good fruit. Every tree that does not bear good fruit is cut down and thrown into the fire. So then, you will know them by their fruits. The good man out of the good treasure of his heart brings forth what is good; and the evil man out of the evil treasure brings forth what is evil; for his mouth speaks from that which fills his heart. Not everyone who says to Me, 'Lord, Lord,' will enter the kingdom of heaven; but he who does the will of My Father who is in heaven. Many will say to Me on that day, 'Lord, Lord, did we not prophesy in Your name, and in Your name cast out demons, and in Your name perform many miracles?' And then I will declare to them, 'I never knew you; depart from Me, you who practice lawlessness.' Therefore everyone who hears these words of Mine, and acts upon them, may be compared to a wise man, who laid a foundation and built his house upon the rock. And the rain descended, and the floods came, and the winds blew, and burst against that house; and yet it did no fall, for it had been founded upon the rock. And everyone who hears these words of Mine, and does not act upon them, will be like a foolish man, who built his house upon the sand without any foundation. And the rain descended, and the floods came, and the winds blew, and burst against that house; and it fell, and great was its fall." The result was that when Jesus had finished these word, the multitudes were amazed at His teaching; for He was teaching them as one having authority, and not as their scribes.

CHAPTER FOURTEEN

When He had completed all His discourse in the hearing of the people, He came down from the mountain. Great multitudes followed Him. He went to Capernaum. Now a certain centurion's slave, who was highly regarded by him was paralyzed, and in great pain, and about to die. When he heard about Jesus, he sent some Jewish elders asking Him to come and save the life of his slave. When they had come to Jesus, they earnestly entreated Him saying, "He is worthy for You to grant this to him; for he loves our nation, and it was he who built us our synagogue." He said to him, "I will come and heal him." Now Jesus started on His way with them; and when He was already not far from the house, the centurion sent friends, saying to Him, "Lord, do not trouble Yourself further, for I am not fit for You to come under my roof; for this reason I did not even consider myself worthy to come to You, but just say the word, and my servant will be healed. For indeed, I am a man under authority, with soldiers under me; and I say to this one, 'Go!' and he goes; and to another, 'Come!' and he comes; and to my slave, 'Do this!' and he does it." When Jesus heard this, He marveled at him, and turned and said to the multitude that was following Him, "Truly, I say to you, not even in Israel have I found such great faith. And I say to you, that many shall come from east and west, and recline at table with Abraham, and Isaac, and Jacob, in the kingdom of heaven; but the sons of the kingdom shall be cast out into the outer darkness; in that place there shall be weeping and gnashing of teeth." Jesus said to the centurion's friends. "Go your way; let it be done as he has believed."

The servant was healed that very hour. When those who had been sent returned to the house, they found the slave in good health.

It came about soon afterwards, that He went to a city called Nain; and His disciples were going along with Him accompanied by a large multitude. Now as he approached the gate of the city, behold, a dead man was being carried out, the only son of his mother, and she was a widow; and a sizable crowd from the city was with her. When the Lord saw her, He felt compassion for her, and said to her, "Do not weep." He came up and touched the coffin; and the bearers came to a halt. He said, "Young man, I say to you, arise!" The dead man sat up, and began to speak. Jesus gave him back to his mother. Fear gripped them all, and they began glorifying God, saying, "A great prophet has arisen among us!" and, "God has visited His people!" This report concerning Him went out all over Judea, and in all the surrounding district.

CHAPTER FIFTEEN

N ow when John was in prison and heard of the works of Christ, he sent word by his disciples, and said to Him, "Are You the Coming One, or shall we look for someone else?" Jesus answered and said to them, "Go and report to John the things which you hear and see; the blind receive sight and the lame walk, the lepers are cleansed and the deaf hear, and the dead are raised up, and the poor have the gospel preached to them. And blessed is he who keeps from stumbling over Me." And as these were going away, Jesus began to say to the multitudes concerning John, "What did you go out into the wilderness to look at? A reed shaken by the wind? But what did you go out to see? A man dressed in soft clothing? Behold, those who wear soft clothing are in kings palaces. But, why did you go out? To see a prophet? Yes, I tell you, and one who is more than a prophet. This is the one about whom it was written, 'Behold, I send My messenger before Your face, who will prepare Your way before You.' Truly, I say to you, among those born of women there has not arisen anyone greater than John the Baptist; yet he who is least in the kingdom of heaven is greater than he. And from the days of John the Baptist until now the kingdom of heaven suffers violence, and violent men take it by force. For all the prophets and the Law prophesied until John. And if you care to accept it, he himself is Elijah, who was to come. He who has ears to hear, let him hear. But to what shall I compare this generation? It is like children sitting in the market places, who call out to the other children, and say, 'We played the flute for you, and you did not dance; we sang a dirge, and you did not mourn.' For John came neither eating nor drinking, and they say 'He has a demon!' The Son of Man came eating and drinking, and they say, 'Behold, a gluttonous man and drunkard, a friend of tax-gatherers and sinners!' Yet wisdom is vindicated by his deeds."

CHAPTER SIXTEEN

Now one of the Pharisees was requesting Him to dine with him. And He entered the Pharisee's house, and reclined at table. Behold, there was a woman in the city who was a sinner; and when she learned that He was reclining at table in the Pharisees's house, she brought an alabaster vial of perfume, and standing behind Him at His feet, weeping, she began to wet His feet with her tears, and kept wiping them with the hair of her head, and kissing His feet, and anointing them with the perfume. Now when the Pharisee who had invited Him saw this, he said to himself, "If this man were a prophet He would know who and what sort of person this woman is who is touching Him, that she is a sinner." Jesus answered and said to him, "Simon, I have something to say to you." He replied, "Say it, Teacher." "A certain moneylender had two debtors; one owed five hundred denarii, and the other fifty. When they were unable to repay, he graciously forgave them both. Which of them therefore will love him more?" Simon answered and said, "I suppose the one whom he forgave more." And he said to him, "You have judged correctly." Turning toward the woman, He said, "Do you see this woman? I entered your house, you gave Me no water for My feet, but she has wet My feet with her tears, and wiped them with her hair. You gave Me no kiss; but she, since the time I came in, has not ceased to kiss My feet. You did not anoint My head with oil, but she anointed My feet with perfume. For this reason I say to you, her sins, which are many, have been forgiven, for she loved much; but he who is forgiven little, loves little." He said to her, "Your sins have been forgiven." And those who were reclining at table with Him began to say to themselves, "Who is this man who even forgives sins?" He said to the woman, "Your faith has saved you; go in peace."

It came about soon afterwards, that He began going about from one city and village to another, proclaiming and preaching the kingdom of God; and the twelve were with Him, also some women who had been healed of evil spirits and sicknesses; Mary who was called Magdalene, from whom seven demons had gone out, and Joanna the wife of Chuza, Herod's steward, and Susanna, and many others who were contributing to their support out of their private means.

Then there was brought to Him a demon-possessed man who was blind and dumb, and He healed him, so that the dumb man spoke and saw. All the multitudes were amazed, and began to say, "This man cannot be the Son of David, can he?" But when the Pharisees heard it, they said, "This man casts out demons only by Beelzebub the ruler of the demons." He know their thoughts, and said to them, "How can Satan cast out Satan? Any kingdom divided against itself is laid waste; and a house divided against itself falls. And if Satan also is divided against himself, how shall his kingdom stand? For you say that I cast out demons by Beelzebub. And if I by Beelzebub cast out demons, by whom do your sons cast them out? Consequently they shall be your judges. But if I cast out demons by the finger of God, then the kingdom of God has come upon you. But no one can enter the strong man's house and plunder his property unless he first binds the strong man, and then he will plunder his house.

Truly I say to you, all sins shall be forgiven the sons of men, and whatever blasphemies they utter; but whoever blasphemes against the Holy Spirit never has forgiveness, but is guilty of an eternal sin. He who is not with Me is against Me; and he who does not gather with Me, scatters. You brood of viper, how can you, being evil, speak what is good? For the mouth speaks out of that which fills the heart. The good man out of his good treasure brings forth what is good; and the evil man out of his evil treasure brings forth what is evil. And I say to you, that every careless word that men shall speak, they shall render account for it in the day of judgment. For by your words you shall be justified, and by your words you shall be condemned." Some of the scribes and

Pharisees, to test Him, were demanding of Him a sign from heaven. He answered and said to them, "An evil and adulterous generation craves for a sign; and yet no sign shall be given to it but the sign of Jonah the prophet; for just as Jonah was three days and three nights in the belly of the sea monster, so shall the Son of Man be three days and three nights in the heart of the earth. The men of Nineveh shall stand up with this generation at the judgment, and shall condemn it because they repented at the preaching Jonah; and behold, something greater than Jonah is here. The Queen of the South shall rise up with this generation at the judgment and shall condemn it, because she came from the ends of the earth to hear the wisdom of Solomon; and behold, something greater than Solomon is here." It came about while He said these things, one of the women in the crowd raised her voice, and said to Him, "Blessed is the womb that bore You, and the breasts at which You nursed." But He said, "On the contrary, blessed are those who hear the word of God, and observe it." As the crowds were increasing, He began to say, "Now when the unclean spirit goes out of a man, it passed through waterless places, seeking rest, and does not find it. Then it says, 'I will return to my house from which I came'; and when it comes, it finds it unoccupied, swept, and put in order. Then it goes, and takes along with it seven other spirits more wicked than itself, and they go in and live there; and the last state of that man becomes worse than the first. That is the way it will also be with this evil generation."

His Mother came to Him and His brothers also, and they were unable to get to Him because of the crowd. And it was reported to Him, "Your Mother and your brothers are standing outside, wishing to see You." He answered and said to the them, "My Mother and My brothers are these who hear the word of God and do it."

CHAPTER SEVENTEEN

Now when he had spoken, a Pharisee asked Him to have lunch with him; and He went in, and reclined at table. When the Pharisee saw it, he was surprised that He had not first ceremonially washed before the meal. But the Lord said to him, "Now you Pharisees clean the outside of the cup and of the platter; but inside of you, you are full of robbery and wickedness. You foolish ones, did not He who made the outside make the inside also? But give that which is within as charity, and then all things are clean for you. But woe to you Pharisees! For you pay tithe of mint and rue and every kind of garden herb, and yet disregard justice and the love of God: but these are the things you should have done without neglecting the others. Woe to you Pharisees! For you love the front seats in the synagogues, and the respectful greetings in the market places. Woe to you! For you are like concealed tombs, and the people who walk over them are unaware of it." One of the lawyers said to Him in reply, "Teacher, when You say this, You insult us too." But He said, "Woe to you lawyers as well! For you weigh men down with burdens hard to bear, while you yourselves will not even touch the burdens with one of your fingers. Woe to you! For you build the tombs of the prophets, and it was your fathers who killed them. Consequently, you are witnesses and approve the deeds of your fathers; because it was they who killed them, and you build their tombs. For this reason also the wisdom of God said, 'I will send to them prophets and apostles, and some of them they will kill and some they will persecute, in order that the blood of all the prophets, shed since the foundation of the world, may be charged against this generation, from the blood of Abel to the blood of Zechariah, who perished between the altar and the house of God; yes, I tell you, it shall be charged against this generation.' Woe to you lawyers! For you have taken away the key of knowledge; you did not enter in yourselves, and those who were entering in you hindered." When He left there, the scribes and the Pharisees began to be very hostile with Him, and plotting against Him.

CHAPTER EIGHTEEN

So many thousands of the multitude had gathered together that they were stepping on one another. He began say to His disciples first of all, "Beware of the leaven of the Pharisees, which is hypocrisy. But there is nothing covered up that will not be revealed, and hidden that will not be known. Accordingly whatever you have said in the dark shall be heard in the light, and what you have whispered in the inner rooms shall be proclaimed upon the housetops. I say to you, My friends do not be afraid of those who kill the body, and after that have no more that they can do. But I will warn you whom to fear; fear the one who after he has killed has authority to cast into hell; yes, I tell you, fear him! Are not five sparrows sold for two cents? And yet not one of them is forgotten before God. Indeed the very hairs of your head are all numbered. Do not fear; you are of more value than many sparrows. I say to you, everyone who confesses Me before men, the Son of Man shall confess him also before the angels of God; but he who denies Me before men shall be denied before the angels of God. And everyone who will speak a word against the Son of Man, it shall be forgiven him; but he who blasphemes against the Holy Spirit, it shall not be forgiven him. And when they bring you before the synagogues and the rulers and the authorities, do not become anxious about how or what you should speak in your defense, or what you should say; for the Holy Spirit will teach you in that very hour what you ought to say."

Someone in the crowd said to Him, "Teacher, tell my brother to divide the family inheritance with me." He said to him, "Man, who appointed Me a judge or arbiter over you?" He said to them, "Beware, and be on your guard against every form of greed: for not even when one has an abundance does his life consist of his possessions." He told them a parable, saying, "The land of a certain rich man was very productive. He began reasoning to himself, saying, 'What shall I do, since I have no place to store my crops?' And he said, 'This is what I will do; I will tear down my barns and build larger ones, and there I will store all my grain and my goods. And I will say to my soul, "Soul, you have many goods laid up for many years to come; take your ease, eat, drink and be merry." But God said to him, 'You fool! This very night your soul is required of you; and now who will own what you have prepared?' So is the man who lays up treasure for himself, and is not rich toward God."

One of His disciples said to Him, "Lord teach us to pray just as John also taught his disciples." He said to them, "When you pray, say; Our Father who art in heaven, hollowed be Thy name. Thy kingdom come. Thy will be done, on earth as it is in heaven. Give us this day our daily bread. And forgive us our debts, as we also have forgiven our debtors. And lead us not into temptation. For Thine is the kingdom, and the power, and the glory, forever, Amen."

Jesus continued to teach them, "Be like men who are waiting for their master when he returns from the wedding feast, so that they may immediately open the door to him when he comes and knocks. Blessed are those slaves whom the master shall find on the alert when he comes; truly I say to you, that he will gird himself to serve, and have them recline at table, and will come up and wait on them. Whether he comes in the second watch, or even in the third, and finds them so, blessed are those slaves. And be sure of this, that if the head of the house had known at what hour the thief was coming, he would not have allowed his house to be broken into. You too, be ready; for the Son of Man is coming at an hour that you do not expect." And Peter said, "Lord are You addressing this parable to us, or to everyone else as well?" The Lord said, "Who then is the faithful and sensible steward, whom his master will put in charge of his servants, to give them their rations at the proper time? Blessed is that slave whom his master finds so doing when he comes. Truly I say to you, that he will put him in charge of all his possessions. But if that slave says in his heart, 'My master will be a long time in coming.' And begins to beat the slaves, both men and women, and eat and drink and get drunk; the master of the slave will come on a day when he does not expect him, and at an hour he does not know, and will cut him in pieces, and assign him a place with the unbelievers. And the slave who knew his master's will and did not get ready or act in accord with his will, shall receive many lashes, but the one who did not know it, and committed deeds worthy of a flogging, will receive but few. And from everyone who has been given much shall much be required; and to whom they entrusted much, of him they will ask all the more. I have come to cast fire upon the earth; and how I wish it were already kindled! But I have a baptism to undergo, and how distressed I am until it is accomplished!" He was also saying to multitudes, "When you see a cloud rising in the west, immediately you say, 'A shower is coming,' and so it turns out. And when you see a south, wind blowing, you say, 'It will be a hot day,' and it turns out that way. You hypocrites! You know how to analyze the appearance of the earth and the sky, but why do you not analyze this present time? And why do you not even on your own initiative judge what is right?"

CHAPTER NINETEEN

H e began telling this parable: "A certain man has a fig tree which had been planted in his vineyard; and he came looking for fruit on it, and did not find any. He said to the vineyard keeper, 'Behold, for three years I have come looking for fruit on this fig tree without finding any. Cut it down! Why does it even use up the ground?' And he answered and said to him, 'Let it alone, sir, for this year too, until I dig around it and put in fertilizer; and if it bears fruit next year, fine. But did not, and cut it down.'"

He spoke by way of this parable: "Listen to this! Behold, the sower went out to sow his seed; and as he sowed, some fell beside the road: and it was trampled under foot, and the birds of the air devoured it. And other seed fell on rocky soil, and as soon as it grew up, it withered away, because it had no moisture. And other seed fell among the thorns; and the thorns grew up with it, and choked it out. And other seed fell into the good ground, and grew up, and produced a crop a hundred times as great." As He said these things, He would call out, "He who has ears to hear, let him hear." His disciples began questioning Him as to what this parable might be. Jesus said, "Do you not understand this parable? How will you understand all the parables? To you it is granted to know the mysteries of the kingdom of God, but to the rest it is in parables; in order that seeing they may not see, and hearing they may not understand. In their case the prophecy of Isaiah is being fulfilled, which says, 'You will keep on hearing, but will not understand; and you will keep on seeing, but will not perceive; for the heart of this people has become dull, and with their ears they scarcely hear, and they have closed their eyes lest they should see with their eyes, and hear with their ears, and understand with their heart and turn again, and I should heal them.' But blessed are your eyes, because they see; and your ears, because they hear. For truly I say to you, that many prophets and righteous men desired to see what you see, and did not see it; and to hear what you hear, and did not hear it. Now the parable is this, the seed is the word of God. And those beside the road are those who have heard; then the devil comes and takes away the word from their heart, so that they may not believe and be saved. And those on the rocky soil are those who, when they hear, receive the word with joy; and theses have no firm root; they believe for a while, and in time of temptation fall away. And the seed which fell among the thorns, these are the ones who have heard, and as they go on their way they are choked with worries and riches and pleasures of this life, and bring no fruit to maturity. And the seed in the good ground, theses are the ones who have heard the word in an honest and good heart, and hold it fast, and bear fruit with perseverance.

Now no one after lighting a lamp covers it over with a container, or puts it under a bed; but he puts it on a lampstand, in order that those who come in may see the light. For nothing is hidden that shall not become evident, nor anything secret that shall not be known and come to light. Therefore take care how you listen. By your standard of measure it shall be measured to you; and more shall be given you besides. For whoever has, to him shall more be given; and whoever does not have, even what he has shall be taken away from him." He said, "The kingdom of God is like a man who casts seed upon the ground; and goes to bed at night and gets up by day, and the seed sprouts up and grows, how, he himself does not know. The earth produces crops by itself; first the blade, then the head, then the mature grain in the head. But when the crop permits, he immediately puts in the sickle, because the harvest has come."

He presented another parable to them, saying, "The kingdom of heaven may be compared to a man who sowed good seed in his field. But while the man was sleeping, his enemy came and sowed tares also among the wheat, and went away. But when the wheat sprang up and bore grain, then the tares became evident also. The slaves of the landowner came and said to him, 'Sir, did you not sow good seed in your field? How then does it have tares?' He said to them 'An enemy has done this!' The slaves said to him, 'Do you want us, then, to go and gather them up?' But he said, 'No, lest while you are gathering up the tares, you may root up the wheat with them. Allow both to grow together until the harvest; and in the time of the harvest I will say to the reapers, "First gather up the tares and bind them in bundles to burn them up; but gather the wheat into my barn."' Then he left the multitudes, and went into the house. His disciples came to Him, saying, "Explain to us the parable of the tares of the field." He answered and said, "The one who sows the good seed is the Son of Man, and his field is the world; and as for the good seed, these are the sons of the kingdom; and the tares are the sons of the evil one; and the enemy who sowed them is the devil, and the harvest is the end of the age; and the reapers are angels. Therefore just as the tares are gathered up and burned with fire, so shall it be at the end of the age. The Son of Man will send forth His angels, and they will gather out of His kingdom all stumbling blocks, and those who commit lawlessness, and will cast them into the furnace of fire; in that place there shall be weeping and gnashing of teeth. Then the righteous will shine forth as the sun in the kingdom of their Father, He who has ears, let him hear. The kingdom of heaven is like a treasure hidden in the field, which a man found and hid; and from joy over it he goes and sells all that he has, and buys that field. Again, the kingdom of heaven is like a merchant seeking fine pearls, and upon finding one pearl of great value, he went and sold all that he had, and bought it. Again, the kingdom of heaven is like a dragnet cast into the sea, and gathering fish of every kind; and when it was filled, they drew it up on the beach; and they sat down, and gathered the good fish into containers, but the bad they threw away. So it will be at the end of the age; the angels shall come forth, and take out the wicked from among the righteous, and will cast them into the furnace of fire; there shall be weeping and gnashing of teeth. Have you understood all these thing?" They said to Him, "Yes."

Therefore every scribe who has become a disciple of the kingdom of heaven is like a head of a household, who brings forth out of his treasure things new and old." He said, "What is the kingdom of God like, and to what shall I compare it? It is like a mustard seed, which man took and threw into his own garden. Though it is smaller than all the seeds that are upon the ground, it grew and became larger than all the garden plants and forms larger branches. So that the birds of the air can nest under its shade." Again He said, "To what shall I compare the kingdom of God? It is like leaven which a woman took and hid in three pecks of meal, until it was all leavened." And with many such parables He was speaking the word to them as they were able to hear it; and He was not speaking to them without parables; so that what was spoken through the prophet might be fulfilled saying, "I will open My mouth in parables; I will utter things hidden since the foundation of the world," but He was explaining everything privately to His own disciples.

Chapter Twenty

O n that day, when evening had come, He said to them, "Let us go over to the other side." A certain scribe came and said to Him, "Teacher, I will follow you wherever You go." Jesus said to him, "The foxes have holes, and birds of the air have nests; but the Son of Man has nowhere to lay His head." Another of the disciples said to Him, "Lord, permit me first to go and bury my father." Jesus said to him, "Follow Me; and allow the dead to bury their own dead." Leaving the multitudes, they took Him along with them, just as He was, in the boat, and other boats were with Him. There arose a fierce gale of wind, and the waves were breaking over the boat so much that the boat was already filling up. He Himself was in the stern, asleep on the cushion; and they awoke Him and said to Him, "Teacher, do you not care that we are perishing?" Being aroused, He rebuked the wind and said to the sea, "Hush, be still." The wind died down and it became perfectly calm. He said to them, "Why are you so timid? How is it that you have no faith?" They became very much afraid and said to one another, "Who then is this, that even the wind and the sea obey Him?" They sailed to country of the Gerasenes, which is opposite Galilee.

When He had come out of the boat, immediately a man from the tombs with an unclean spirit met Him, and he had his dwelling among the tombs. No one was able to bind him any more, even with a chain; because he had often been bound with shackles and chains, chains had been torn apart by him, and shackles broken in pieces, and no one was strong enough to subdue him. Constantly night and day, among the tombs and in the mountains, he was crying out and gashing himself with stones. Seeing Jesus from a distance, he ran up and bowed down before Him; and crying out with a loud voice, he said, "What do I have to do with You, Jesus, Son of the Most High God? I implore You by God, do not torment me!" For He had been saying to him, "Come out of the man, you unclean spirit?" He was asking him, "What is your name?" He said to Him, "My name is Legion; for we are many." He began to entreat Him earnestly not to send them into the abyss. Now there was a big herd of swine feeding there on the mountain side. They entreated Him, saying, "Send us into the swine so that we may enter them." He gave them permission. Coming out, the unclean spirits entered the swine; and the herd rushed down the steep bank into the sea, about two thousand of them; and they were drowned in the sea. Those who tended them ran away and reported it in the city and out in the country. The people came to see what it was that had happened. They came to Jesus and observed the man who had been demon possessed sitting down, clothed and in his right mind, the very man who had had the "legion"; and they became frightened. Those who had seen it described to them how it had happened to the demon possessed man, and all about the swine. They began to entreat Him to depart from the region. As He was getting into the boat, the man who had been demon possessed was entreating Him that he might accompany Him. He did not let him, but He said to him, "Go home to your people and report to them what great things the Lord has done for you, and how He had mercy on you." The man went off and began to proclaim in Decapolis what great things Jesus had done for him; and everyone marveled.

Jesus crossed over again in the boat to the other side, a great multitude gathered about him. One of the synagogue officials named Jairus came up, and upon seeing Him, fell at His feet, and entreated Him earnestly, saying, "My little daughter is at the point of death; please come and lay Your hands on her, that she may get well and live." He went off with him; and a great multitude was following Him and pressing in on Him. A woman who had had a hemorrhage for twelve years, and had endured much at the hands of many physicians, and had spent all that she had was not helped at all, but rather had grown worse, after hearing about Jesus, came up in the crowd behind Him, and touched His cloak. For she thought, "If I just touch His garments, I shall get well." Immediately the flow of her blood was dried up; and she felt in her body that she was healed of her affliction. Immediately Jesus, perceiving in Himself that the power proceeding from Him had gone forth, turned around in the crowd and said, "Who touched My garments?" His disciples said to Him, "You see the multitude pressing in on You, and You say, "Who touched Me?" Jesus said, "Some one did touch Me, for I was aware that power had gone out of Me." He looked around to see the woman who had done this. But the woman fearing and trembling, aware of what had happened to her, came and fell down before Him, and told Him the whole truth. He said to her, "Daughter, your faith had made you well; go in peace, and be healed of your affliction." While He was still speaking, they came from the house of the synagogue official, saying, "Your daughter has died; why trouble the Teacher any more." Jesus, overhearing what was being spoken, said to the synagogue official, "Do not be afraid any longer, only believe." He allowed no one to follow with Him, except Peter and James and John the brother of James. They came to the house of the synagogue official; and He beheld a commotion, and people loudly weeping and wailing. Entering in, He said to them, "Why make a commotion and weep? The child has not died, but is asleep." They were laughing at Him. But putting them all out, He took along the child's father and mother and His own companions, and entered the room where the child was. Taking the child by the hand, He said to her, "Talitha kum!" (which translated means, "Little girl, I say to you, arise!") Immediately the girl got up and began to walk; for she was twelve years old. Immediately they were completely astounded. He gave them strict orders that no one should know about this; and He said that something should be given her to eat.

As Jesus passed on from there, two blind men followed Him, crying out, and saying, "Have mercy on us, Son of David!" After He had come into the house, the blind three men came up to Him, and Jesus said to them, "Do you believe that I am able to do this?" They said to Him, "Yes, Lord." He touched their eyes, saying, "Be it done to you according to your faith." Their eyes were opened. Jesus sternly warned them, saying, "See here, let no one know about this!" But they went out, and spread the news about Him in all that land. As they were going out, behold, a dumb man, demon possessed, was brought to Him. After the demon was cast out, the dumb man spoke; and the multitudes marveled, saying, "Nothing like this was ever seen in Israel." The Pharisees were saying, "He casts out the demons by the ruler of the demons." Jesus was going about all the cities and the villages, teaching in their synagogues, and proclaiming the gospel of the kingdom, and healing every kind of disease and every kind of sickness. Seeing the multitudes, He felt compassion for them, because they were distressed and downcast like sheep without a shepherd. He said to His disciples, "The harvest is plentiful, but the workers are few. Therefore beseech the Lord of the harvest to send out workers into His harvest."

CHAPTER TWENTY ONE

He went out from there, and He came into His hometown; and His disciples followed Him. When the Sabbath had come, He began to teach in the synagogue; and the many listeners were astonished, saying, "Where did this man get these things, and what is this wisdom given to Him, and such miracles as these performed by His hands? Is not this the carpenter's son, the son of Mary, and brother of James, and Joses, and Judas, and Simon? Are not His sisters here with us?" They took offense of Him. Jesus said to them, "A prophet is not without honor except in his hometown and among his own relatives and in his own household." He could not do miracles there because of their unbelief, except that He laid His hands upon a few sick people and healed them. He wondered at their unbelief. He was going around the villages teaching.

He summoned the twelve and began to send them out in pairs: the names of the twelve apostles are these; the first, Simon, who is called Peter, and Andrew his brother; and James the son of Zebedee, and John his brother; Philip and Bartholomew; Thomas and Matthew the tax gatherer; James the son of Alphaeus, and Thaddaeus; Simon the Cananaean, and Judas Iscariot. He was giving them authority over the unclean spirits; and He instructed them saying, "Do not go in the way of the gentiles, and do not enter any city of the Samaritans: but rather go to the lost sheep of the house of Israel. And as you go, preach, saying, 'The kingdom of heaven is at hand.' Heal the sick, raise the dead, cleanse the lepers, cast out demons; freely you received, freely give. Do not acquire gold, or silver, or copper for you money belt; or a bag for your journey, or even two tunics, or sandals, or a staff; for the worker is worthy of his support. And onto whatever city or village you enter, inquire who is worthy in it; and abide there until you go away. As you enter the house, give it your greeting. If the house is worthy, let your greeting of peace come upon it; but if it is not worthy, let your greeting of peace return to you. And whoever does not receive you, nor heed your words, as you go out of that house or that city, shake off the dust of your feet. Behold, I send you out as sheep in the midst of wolves; therefore be shrewd as serpents, and innocent as doves. But beware of men; for they will deliver you up to the court, and scourge you in their synagogues; and you shall even be brought before governors and kings for My sake, as a testimony to them and to the Gentiles. But when they deliver you up, do not become anxious about how or what you will speak; for it shall be given you in that hour what you are to speak. For it is not you who speak, but it is the Spirit of your Father who speaks in you. And brother will deliver up brother to death, and father his child; and children will rise up against parents, and cause them to be put to death. You will be hated by all on account of My name, but it is the one who has endured to the end who will be saved. But whenever they persecute you in this city, flee to the next; for truly I say to you, you shall not finish going through the cities of Israel, until the Son of Man comes.

A disciple is not above his teacher, nor a slave above his master. It is enough for the disciple that he become as his teacher, and slave as his master. If they have called the head of the house Beelzebub, how much the members of his household! Therefore do not fear them. He who loves father or mother more than Me is not worthy of Me; and he who loves son or daughter more that Me is not worthy of Me. And he who does not take his cross and follow after Me is not worthy of Me. He who had found his life shall lose it, and he who has lost his life for My sake shall find it. He who receives you receives Me, and he who receives Me receives Him who sent Me. He who receives a prophet in the name of a prophet shall receive a prophet's reward; and he who receives a righteous man in the name of a righteous man shall receive a righteous man's reward. And whoever in the name of a disciple gives to one of these little ones even a cup of cold water to drink, truly I say to you he shall not lose his reward." They went out and preached that men should repent. They were casting out many demons and were anointing with oil many sick people and healing them.

CHAPTER TWENTY TWO

King Herod heard all about Jesus, for His name had become well known; and people were saying, "John the Baptist has risen from the dead, and therefore these miraculous powers are a work in Him." Others were saying, "He is Elijah." Others are saying "He is a prophet, like one of the prophets of old." But when Herod hear of it, he kept saying, "John, whom I beheaded, He has risen!" For Herod himself had sent and had John arrested and bound in prison on account of Herodias, the wife of his brother Philip, because he had married her. For John had been saying to Herod, "It is not lawful for you to have your brother's wife." Herodias had a grudge against him and wanted to kill him; and could not do so; for Herod was afraid of John, knowing that he was a righteous and holy man, and kept him safe. A strategic day came when Herod on his birthday gave a banquet for his lords and military commanders and the leading men of Galilee; and when the daughter of Herodias herself came in and danced, she pleased Herod and his dinner quests; and the king said to the girl, "Ask me for whatever you want and I will give it to you." He swore to her, "Whatever you ask of me, I will give it to you; up to half of my kingdom." She went out and said to her mother, "What shall I ask for?" And she said, "The head of John the Baptist." Immediately she came in haste before the king and asked, saying, "I want you to give me right away the head of John the Baptist on a platter." Although the king was very sorry, yet because of his oaths and because of his dinner guest, he was unwilling to refuse her. Immediately the king sent an executioner and commanded him to bring back his head. He went and beheaded him in the prison, and brought his head on a platter, and gave it to the girl; and girl gave it to her mother.

When his disciples heard about this, they came and took away his body and laid it in a tomb. The apostles gathered together with Jesus; and they reported to Him all that they had done and taught. He said to them, "Come away by yourselves to a lonely place and rest a while." (For there were many people coming and going, and they did not even have time to eat.) And they went away in the boat to a lonely place by themselves. The people saw them going, and many recognized them, they had seen the signs which He was performing on those who were sick, and they ran there together on foot from all the cities, and got there ahead of them.

CHAPTER TWENTY THREE

Now the Passover, the feast of the Jews, was at hand. While disembarking He saw a great multitude, and He felt compassion for them. He began to teach them many things. When it was already quite late, His disciples came up to Him and began saying, "The place is desolate and it is already quite late; send them away so that they may go into the surrounding countryside and villages and buy themselves something to eat." He answered and said to Philip, "You give them something to eat!" This He was saying to test him; for He Himself knew what He was intending to do. Philip said to Him, "Shall we go and spend two hundred denarii on bread and give them something to eat?" He said to them, "How many loaves do you have? Go look!" When they found out, Andrew said, "There is a lad here, who has five barley loaves, and two fish; but what are these for so many people?" He commanded them all to recline by groups on the green grass. They reclined in companies of hundreds and fifties. He took the five loaves and the two fish, and looking up toward heaven, He blessed the food and broke the loaves and He kept giving them to the disciples to set before them; and He divided up the two fish among them all. They all ate and were satisfied. He said to His disciples, "Gather up the leftover fragments that nothing may be lost." They picked up twelve full baskets of the broken pieces, and also of the fish. There were five thousand men who ate the loaves, aside from women and children. When the people saw the sign which He had performed, they said, "This is of a true Prophet who is to come into the world." Jesus perceiving that they were intending to come and take Him by force, to make Him king, withdrew from them.

Immediately He made His disciples get into the boat and go ahead of Him to Capernaum. He went to the mountain by Himself to be alone and pray. It became dark, and the sea began to be stirred up because a strong wind was blowing. When they had rowed about three or four miles, they beheld Jesus walking on the sea and drawing near to the boat; and they were frightened, they supposed that it was a ghost. He said to them, "It is I; do not be afraid." Peter answered Him and said, "Lord, if it is You, command me to come to You on the water." He said, "Come." Peter got out of the boat, and walked on the water and came toward Jesus. But seeing the wind, he became afraid, and beginning to sink, he cried out, saying, "Lord, save me!" Immediately he stretched out His hand and took hold of him, and said to him, "O you of little faith, why did you doubt?" When they got into the boat, the wind stopped. Those who were in the boat worshiped Him, "You are certainly God's Son!" Immediately the boat was at the land to which they were going.

When they had come out of the boat, immediately the people recognized Him, and ran about that whole country and began to carry about on their pallets those were sick, to the place they heard He was. They began to entreat Him that they might just touch the fringe of His cloak; and as many as touched it were cured.

The next day the multitude that stood on the other side of the sea saw that there was no other small boat there, except one, and the Jesus had not entered with His disciples into the boat, but that His disciples had gone away alone. There came other small boats from Tiberias near to the place where they ate the bread after the Lord had given thanks. When the multitude saw that Jesus was not there, nor His disciples, they themselves got into the small boats, and came to Capernaum, seeking Jesus. When they found Him on the other side of the sea, they said to Him, "Rabbi, when did You get here?" Jesus answered them and said, "Truly, truly, I say to you, you seek Me, not because you saw signs, but because you ate of the loaves, and were filled. Do not work for the food which perishes, but for the food which endures to eternal life, which the Son of Man shall give to you, for on Him the Father, even God, has set His seal."

They said to Him, "What shall we do, that we may work the works of God?" Jesus answered and said to them, "This is the work of God, that you believe in Him whom He has sent." They said to Him, "What then do You do for a sign, that we may see, and believe You? What work do you perform? Our fathers ate the manna in the wilderness: as it is written, 'He gave them bread out of heaven to eat.'" Jesus said to them, "Truly, truly, I say to you, it is not Moses who has given you the bread out of heaven, but it is My Father who gives you the true bread out of heaven. For the bread of God is that which comes down out of heaven, and gives life to the world." They said to Him, "Lord, evermore give us the bread." Jesus said to them, "I am the bread of life; he who comes to Me shall not hunger, and he who believes in Me shall never thirst. But I said to you, that you have seen Me, and yet do not believe. All that the Father gives Me shall come to Me; and the one who comes to Me I will certainly not cast out. For I have come down from heaven, not to do My own will, but the will of Him who sent Me. And this is the will of Him who sent Me, that of all that He has given Me I lose nothing, but raise it up on the last day. For this is the will of My Father, that every one who beholds the Son, and believes in Him, may have eternal life; and I Myself will raise him up on the last day." The Jews were grumbling about Him, because He said, "I am the bread that came down out of heaven." They were saying, "Is not this Jesus, the son of Joseph, whose father and mother we know? How does He now say, 'I have come down out of heaven?'" Jesus answered and said to them, "Do not grumble among yourselves. No one can come to Me, unless the Father who sent Me draws him; and I will raise him up on the last day. It is written in the prophets, 'And they shall all be taught of God.' Every one who had heard and learned from the Father, come to Me. Not that any man has seen the Father, except the One who is from God; He has seen the Father. Truly, truly, I say to you, he who believes has eternal life. I am the bread of life. Your fathers ate the manna in the wilderness, and they died. This is the bread which comes down out of heaven, so that one may eat of it and not die. I am the living bread that came down out of heaven; if any one eats of this bread, he shall live forever; and the bread also which I shall give for the life of the world is My flesh." The Jews began to argue with one another, saying, "How can this man give us His flesh to eat?" Jesus said to them, "Truly, Truly, I say to you, unless you eat the flesh of the Son of Man and drink His blood, you have no life in yourselves. He who eats My flesh and drinks My blood has eternal life; and I will raise him up on the last day. For My flesh is true food, and My blood is true drink. He who eats My flesh and drinks My blood abides in Me, and I in him. As the living Father sent Me, and I live because of the Father, so he who eats Me, he also shall live because of Me. This is the bread which came down out of heaven; not as the fathers ate, and died, he who eats this bread shall live forever."

These things He said in the synagogue, as He taught in Capernaum. Many of His disciples, when they heard this said, "This is a difficult statement; who can listen to it?" Jesus, conscious that His disciples grumbled at this, said to them, "Does this cause you to stumble. What then if you should behold the Son of Man ascending where He was before. It is the Spirit who gives life; the flesh profits nothing; the words that I have spoken to you are spirit and are life. But there are some of you who do not believe." For Jesus knew from the beginning who they were who did not believe, and who it was that would betray Him. He was saying, "For this reason I have said to you, that no one can come to Me, unless it has been granted him from the Father." As a result of this many of His disciples withdrew, and were not walking with Him anymore. Jesus said to the twelve, "You do not want to go away also, do you?" Simon Peter answered Him, "Lord, to whom shall we go? You have words of eternal life. And we have believed and have come to know that You are the Holy One of God." Jesus answered them, "Did I Myself not choose you, the twelve, and yet one of you is a devil?" Now He meant Judas the son of Simon Iscariot, for he, one of the twelve, was going to betray Him.

Chapter Twenty Four

The Pharisees and some of the scribes gathered together around Him when they had come from Jerusalem, and had seen that some of His disciples were eating their bread with impure hands, that is, unwashed. (For the Pharisees and all the Jews do not eat unless they carefully wash their hands; thus observing the traditions of the elders; and when they come from the market place, they do not eat unless they cleanse themselves; and there are many other things which they have received in order to observe, such as the washing of cups and pitchers and copper pots.) The Pharisees and the scribes asked Him, "Why do your disciples not walk according to the tradition of the elder, but eat their bread with impure hands?" He said to them, "Rightly did Isaiah prophesy of you hypocrites, as it is written, 'This people honor Me with their lips, but their heart is far away from Me, but in vain do they worship Me, teaching as doctrines the precepts of men.' Neglecting the commandment of God, you hold to the tradition of men." He was also saying to them, "You nicely set aside the commandment of God in order to keep your tradition. For Moses said, 'Honor your father and your mother'; and, 'He who speaks evil of father or mother, let him be put to death'; but you say, 'If a man says to his father or his mother, anything of mine you might have been helped by is Coban (that is say, given to God), you no longer permit him to do anything for his father or mother; thus invalidating the word of God by your tradition which you have handed down; and you do many things such as that."

Summoning the multitude again, He began saying to them, "Listen to Me, all of you and understand; there is nothing outside the man which going into him can defile him; but the things which proceed out of the mouth of man are what defile the man. If any man has ears to hear, let him hear." When leaving the multitude, He had entered the house, his disciples questioned Him about the parable. He said to them, "Are you too so uncomprehending? Do you not see that whatever goes into the man from outside cannot defile him; because it does not go into his heart, but into his stomach, and is eliminated?" He was saying, "That which proceeds out of the mouth of man, that is what defiles the man. For from within, out of the heart of man, proceed the evil thoughts and fornication, thefts, murders, adulteries, deeds of coveting and wickedness, as well as deceit, sensuality, envy, slander, pride and foolishness. All these evil things proceed from within defile the man."

From there He arose and went away to the region of Tyre. When He had entered a house, He wanted no one to know of it; yet He could not escape notice. But after hearing of Him, a woman immediately came and fell at His feet. Now the woman was a Gentile, of the Syrophoenician race (greek). She began crying out to Him, "Have mercy on me, O Lord, Son of David, my daughter is cruelly demon possessed." She asking Him to cast the demon out of her daughter. He did not answer her a word. His disciples came to Him, saying "Send her away, for she is shouting out after us." He answered and said, "I was sent only to the lost sheep of the house of Israel." She came and began to bow down before Him, saying, "Lord, help me!" He was saying to her, "Let the children be satisfied first, for it is not good to take the children's bread and throw it to the dogs." She answered and said to Him, "Yes, Lord, but even the dogs under the table feed on the children's crumbs." He said to her, "Because of this answer your faith is great; go your way, the demon has gone out of your daughter." Going back to her home, she found the child lying on the bed, the demon having departed.

Again He went out from the region of Tyre, and came through Sidon to the Sea of Galilee, within the region of Decapolis. They brought to Him one who was deaf and spoke with difficulty, and they entreated Him to lay His hand upon him. He took him aside from the multitude by Himself, and put His fingers into his ears, and after spitting, He touched his tongue with the saliva; and looking up to heaven with deep sigh, He said to him, "Ephphatha!" that is, "Be opened!" His ears were opened, and the impediment of the tongue was removed, and he began speaking plainly. He gave him orders not to tell anyone; but the more He ordered them, the more widely they continued to proclaim it. They were utterly astonished, saying "He has done all things well; He makes even the deaf to hear, and the dumb to speak." The great multitudes came to Him, bringing with them those who were lame, crippled, blind, dumb, and many others, and they laid them down at His feet; and He healed them, so that the multitude marveled as they saw the dumb speaking, the crippled restored, and the lame walking, and the blind seeing; and they glorified the God of Israel.

In those days again, when there was a great multitude and they had nothing to eat, He summoned His disciples and said to them, "I feel compassion for the multitude because they have remained with Me now three days, and have nothing to eat; and if I send them away fasting to their home, they will faint on the way; and some of them have come from a distance." His disciples answered Him, "Where will anyone be able to find enough to satisfy these men with bread here in the wilderness?" He was asking them, "How many loaves do you have?" They said, "Seven." He directed the multitude to sit down on the ground; and taking the seven loaves, He gave thanks and broke them, and began giving them to His disciples to serve to them, and they served them to the multitude. They also had a few small fish; and after He had blessed them, He ordered these to be served as well. They ate and were satisfied; and they picked up seven full baskets of what was left over of the broken pieces. About four thousand were there; and He sent them away.

CHAPTER TWENTY FIVE

He entered the boat with His disciples, and came to the district of Dalmanutha. The Pharisees came out and began to argue with Him, seeking from Him a sign from heaven, to test Him. Sighing deeply in His spirit, He said, "Why does this generation seek for a sign? Truly I say to you, an evil and adulterous generation seeks after a sign; no sign shall be given to this generation, except the sign of Jonah." Leaving them, He again embarked and went away to the other side.

The disciples had forgotten to take bread. Jesus said to them, "Watch out and beware of the leaven of the Pharisees and Sadducees." They began to discuss among themselves, saying, "It is because we took no bread." Jesus, aware of this, said, "You men of little faith, why do you discuss among yourselves because you have no bread? Do you not yet understand or remember the five loaves of the five thousand, and how many baskets you took up? Or the seven loaves of the four thousand, and how many baskets you took up? How is it that you do not understand that I did not speak to you concerning bread? But beware of the leaven of the Pharisees and Sadducees." Then they understood that He did not say to beware of the leaven of bread, but of the teaching of Pharisees and Sadducees.

They came to Bethsaida. They brought a blind man to Him, and entreated Him to touch him. Taking the blind man by the hand, He brought him out of the village; and after spitting on his eyes, and laying His hands upon him, He asked him, "Do you see anything?" He looked up and said, "I see men, for I am seeing them like trees, walking about." Then again He laid His hands upon his eyes; and he looked intently and was restored, and began to see everything clearly. He sent him to his home, saying, "Do not even enter the village."

Jesus went out, along with His disciples, to the villages of Caesarea Philippi: and on the way He questioned His disciples, saying to them, "Who do people say that I am?" They told Him, saying, "John the Baptist; and others say Elijah; but still others, one of the prophets of old has risen again." He continued by questioning them, "But who do you say that I am?" Peter answered and said to Him, "Thou art the Christ." Jesus answered and said to him, "Blessed are you, Simon Barjona, because flesh and blood did not reveal this to you, but My Father who is in heaven. And I also say to you that you are Peter, and upon this rock I will build My church; and the gates of Hades shall not overpower it. I will give you the keys of the kingdom of heaven; and whatever you shall bind on earth shall have been bound in heaven, and whatever you shall loose on earth shall have been loosed in heaven." He warned them to tell no one about Him. He began to teach them that the Son of Man must suffer many things and be rejected by the elders, the chief priests and the scribes, be killed, and after three days rise again. He was stating the matter plainly. Peter took Him aside and began to rebuke Him. Turning around and seeing His disciples, He rebuked Peter, and said, "Get behind Me, Satan; for you are not setting your mind on God's interests, but man's." He summoned the multitude with His disciples, and said to them, "If anyone wishes to come after Me, let him deny himself, and take up his cross, and follow Me. For whoever wishes to save his life shall lose it; and whoever loses his life for My sake and the gospel's shall save it. For what does it profit a man to gain the whole world, and forfeit his soul? For what shall a man give in exchange for his soul? For whoever is ashamed of Me and My words in this adulterous and sinful generation, the Son of Man will also be ashamed of him when He comes in the glory of His Father with the holy angels. But I tell you truly, there are some of those standing here who shall not taste death until they see the kingdom of God."

CHAPTER TWENTY SIX

Some eight days after this, it came about that He took along Peter and John and James, and went up to the mountain to pray. While He was praying, the appearance of his face became different, and His clothing became white and gleaming. Behold, two men were talking with Him; and they were Moses and Elijah, who, appearing in glory, were speaking of His departure which He was about to accomplish at Jerusalem. Now Peter and his companions had been overcome with sleep; but when they were fully awake, they saw His glory and the two men standing with Him. It came about, as these were parting from Him, Peter said to Jesus, "Master, it is good for us to be here; and let us make three tabernacles; one for You, and one for Moses, and one for Elijah" not realizing what he was saying. While he was saying this, a cloud formed and began to overshadow them; and they were afraid as they entered the cloud. A voice came out of the cloud, saying, "This is My Son, My Chosen One; listen to Him!" When the disciples heard this, they fell on their faces and were much afraid. Jesus came to them and touched them and said, "Arise, and do not be afraid." When the voice had spoken, Jesus was found alone. As they were coming down from the mountain, Jesus commanded them, saying, "Tell the vision to no one until the Son of Man has risen from the dead." His disciples asked Him, saying, "Why then do the scribes say that Elijah must come first?" He answered and said, "Elijah is coming and will restore all things; but I say to you, that Elijah already came, and they did not recognize him, but did to him whatever they wished. So also the Son of Man is going to suffer at their hands." Then the disciples understood that He had spoken to them about John the Baptist. They kept silent, and reported to no one in those days any of the things which they had seen.

Chapter Twenty Seven

When He came back to the disciples, they saw a large crowd around them, and some scribes arguing with them. Immediately, when the entire crowd saw Him, they were amazed, and began running up to greet Him. He asked them, "What are you discussing with them?" One of the crowd answered Him, "Teacher, I brought You my son, my only boy, possessed with a spirit which makes him mute; and whenever it seizes him, it dashes him to the ground and he foams at the mouth, grinds his teeth, and stiffens out. I begged Your disciples to cast it out, and they could not do it." He answered them, and said, "O unbelieving generation, how long shall I be with you? How long shall I put up with you? Bring him to Me!" They brought the boy to Him. When he saw Him, immediately the spirit threw him into a convulsion, and falling to the ground, he began rolling about and foaming at the mouth. He asked his father, "How long has this been happening to him?" He said, "From childhood. It has often thrown him both into the fire and into the water to destroy him. If You can do anything, take pity on us and help us!" Jesus said to him, "If you can believe! All things are possible to him who believe." Immediately the boy's father cried out and began saying, "I do believe; help me in my unbelief." When Jesus saw that a crowd was rapidly gathering, He rebuked the unclean spirit, saying to it, "You deaf and dumb spirit, I command you, come out of him and do not enter him again." After crying out and throwing him into terrible convulsions, it came out; and the boy became so much like a corpse that most of them said, "He is dead!" Jesus took him by the hand and raised him; and he got up. When He had come into the house, His disciples began questioning Him privately, "Why is it that we could not cast it out?' He said to them, "Because of the littleness of your faith; for truly I say to you, if you have faith as a mustard seed, you shall say to this mountain, 'Move from here to there,' and it shall move; and nothing shall be impossible to you. This kind can not come out by anything but prayer and fasting." They were all amazed at the greatness of God.

CHAPTER TWENTY EIGHT

While they were gathering together in Galilee, Jesus said to them, "Let these words sink into your ears; the Son of Man is going to be delivered into the hands of men; and they will kill Him, and He will be raised again on the third day." They did not understand this statement, it was concealed from them so that they might not perceive it; and they were afraid to ask Him. They were deeply grieved.

When they had come to Capernaum, those who collected the two drachma tax came to Peter, and said, "Does your teacher not pay the two drachma tax?" He said, "Yes." When he came into the house, Jesus spoke to him first, saying, "What do you think, Simon? From whom do the kings of the earth collect customs or poll tax, from their sons or from strangers?" Upon his saying, "From strangers." Jesus said to him, "Consequently the sons are exempt. But, lest we give them offense, go to the sea, and throw in a hook, and take the first fish that comes up; and when you open its mouth, you will find a shekel. Take that and give it to them for you and Me."

When He came into the house, He began to question them, "What were you discussing on the way?" But they kept silent, for on the way they had discussed with one another which of them was the greatest. Sitting down, the disciples asked Jesus, saying, "Who then is greatest in the kingdom of heaven?" He said to them, "If any one wants to be first, he shall be last of all, and servant of all." He called a child to Himself and stood him in their midst, and said, "Truly I say to you, unless you are converted and become like children, you shall not enter the kingdom of heaven. Whoever then humbles himself as this child, he is the greatest in the kingdom of heaven. And whoever receives one such child in My name receives Me; but whoever causes one of these little ones who believe in Me to stumble, it is better for him that a heavy millstone be hung around his neck, and that he be drowned in the depth of the sea. Woe to the world because of its stumbling blocks! For it is inevitable that stumbling blocks come; but woe to that man through whom the stumbling block comes. See that you do not despise one of these little ones, for I say to you, that their angels in heaven continually behold the face of My Father who is in heaven. For the Son of Man has come to save that which was lost. What do you think? If any man has a hundred sheep, and one of them has gone astray, does he not leave the ninety-nine on the mountain and go and search for the one that is straying? And if it turns out that he finds it, truly I say to you, he rejoices over it more than over the ninety-nine which have not gone astray. Thus it is not the will of your Father who is in heaven that one of these little ones perish. If your brother sins, go and reprove him in private; if he listens to you, you have won your brother. But if he does not listen to you, take one or two more with you, so that by the mouth of two or three witness every fact may be confirmed. If he refuses to listen to them, tell it to the church; and if he refuses to listen even to the church, let him be to you as a Gentile and a tax gatherer.

Truly I say to you, whatever you shall bind on earth shall have been bound in heaven; and whatever you loose on earth shall have been loosed in heaven. Again I say to you, that if two of you agree on earth about anything that they may ask, it shall be done for them by My Father who is in heaven. For where two or three have gathered together in My name, there I am in their midst."

John said to Him, "Teacher, we saw someone casting out demons in Your name, and we tried to hinder him because he was not following us." Jesus said, "Do not hinder him, for there is no one who shall perform a miracle in My name, and be able soon afterward to speak evil of Me. For he who is not against us is for us. For whoever gives you a cup of water to drink because of your name as followers of Christ, truly I say to you, he shall not lose his reward.

Then Peter came and said to Him, "Lord, how often shall my brother sin against me and I forgive him? Up to seven times?'" Jesus said to him, "I do not say to you, up to seven times, but up to seventy times seven. For this reason the kingdom of heaven may by compared to a certain king who wished to settle accounts with his slaves. When he had began to settle them, there was brought to him one who owed him ten thousand talents. But since he did not have the means to repay, his lord commanded him to be sold, along with his wife and children and all that he had, and repayment to be made. The slave therefore falling down, prostrated himself before him, saying, 'Have patience with me, and I will repay you everything.' And the lord of that slave felt compassion and released him and forgave him the debt. But that slave went out and found one of his fellow slaves who owed him a hundred denarii; and he seized him and began to choke him, saying, 'Pay back what you owe.' So his fellow slave fell down and began to entreat him, saying, 'Have patience with me and I will repay you.' He was unwilling however, but went and threw him in prison until he should pay back what was owed. So when his fellow slaves saw what had happened, they were deeply grieved and came and reported to their lord all that had happened. Then summoning him, his lord said to him, 'You wicked slave, I forgave you all that debt because you entreated me. Should you not also have had mercy on your fellow slave, even as I had mercy on you?' And his lord, moved with anger, handed him over to the torturers until he should repay all that was owed him. So shall My heavenly Father also do to you, if each of you does no forgive his brother from you heart."

CHAPTER TWENTY NINE

N ow after this the Lord appointed seventy others, and sent them two and two ahead of Him to every city and place where He Himself was going to come. He was saying to them, "The harvest is plentiful, but the laborers are few; therefore beseech the Lord of the harvest to sent out laborers into His harvest. Go your ways; behold, I send you out as lambs in the midst of wolves. Carry no purse, no bag, no shoes; and greet no one on the way. And whatever house you enter, first say, 'Peace be to this house.' If a man of peace is there, your peace will rest upon him; but if not, it will return to you. Stay in that house, eating and drinking what they give you; for the laborer is worthy of his wages. Do not keep moving from house, to house. And whatever city you enter, and they receive you, eat what is set before you; and heal those in it who are sick, and say to them, 'The kingdom of God has come near to you.' But whatever city you enter and they do not receive you, go out into its streets and say, 'Even the dust of your city which clings to our feet, we wipe off in protest against you; yet be sure of this, that the kingdom of God has come near.' I say to you, it will be more tolerable in that day for Sodom, than for that city. Woe to you, Chorazin! Woe to you Bethsaida! For if the miracles had been performed in Tyre and Sidon which occurred in you, they would have repented long ago, sitting in sackcloth and ashes. But it will be more tolerable for Tyre and Sidon in the judgment, than for you. And you, Capernaum, will not be exalted to heaven, will you? You will be brought down to Hades! The one who listens to you listens to Me, and the one who rejects you rejects Me; and he who rejects Me rejects the One who sent Me."

It came about, when the days were approaching for His ascension, that He resolutely set His face to go to Jerusalem; and He sent messengers on ahead of Him. They went, and entered a village of the Samaritans, to make a arrangements for Him. They did not receive Him, because He was journeying with His face toward Jerusalem. When His disciples James and John saw this, they said, "Lord, do You want us to command fire to come down from heaven and consume them?" He turned and rebuked them. They went on to another village.

Chapter Thirty

It came about while He was on the way to Jerusalem, that He was passing between Samaria and Galilee. As He entered a certain village, there met Him ten leprous men, who stood at a distance; and they raised their voices, saying, "Jesus, Master, have mercy on us!" When He saw them, He said to them, "Go and show yourselves to the priest." And it came about that as they were going, they were cleansed. Now one of them, when he saw that he had been healed, turned back, glorifying God with a loud voice, and he fell on his face at His feet, giving thanks to Him. He was a Samaritan. Jesus answered and said, "Were there not ten cleansed? But the nine, where are they? Were none found who turned back to give glory to God, except this foreigner?" He said to him, "Rise, and go your way; your faith has made you well."

After these things Jesus was walking in Galilee; for He was unwilling to walk in Judea, because the Jews were seeking to kill Him. Now the feast of Jews, the Feast of Tabernacles, was at hand. His brothers said to Him, "Depart from here, and go into Judea, that Your disciples also may behold your works which You are doing. For no one does anything in secret, when he himself seeks to be known publicly. If You do these things, show Yourself to the world." For not even His brothers were believing in Him. Jesus said to them, "My time is not yet at hand; but your time is always opportune. The world cannot hate you; but it hates Me, because I testify of it, that its deeds are evil. Go up to the feast yourselves; I do not go up to this feast because My time has not yet fully come." Having said these things to them, He stayed in Galilee. But when His brothers had gone up to the feast, then He Himself also went up, not publicly, but as it were, in secret. The Jews were seeking Him at the feast, and were saying, "Where is He?" There was much grumbling among the multitudes concerning Him; some were saying, "He is a good man" ; others were saying, "No, on the contrary, He leads the multitude astray." Yet no one was speaking openly of Him for fear of the Jews. But when it was now the midst of the feast Jesus went up into the temple, and began to teach. The Jews were marveling, saying, "How has this man become learned, having never been educated?" Jesus answered them, and said, "My teaching is not Mine, but His who sent Me. If any man is willing to do His will, he shall know of the teaching, whether it is of God, or whether I speak from Myself. He who speaks from himself seeks his own glory; but He who is seeking the glory of the one who sent Him, He is true, and there is no unrighteousness in Him. Did not Moses give you the law, and yet none of you carries out the law? Why do you seek to kill Me?" The multitude answered, "You have a demon! Who seeks to kill You?" Jesus answered and said to them, "I did one good deed, and you all marvel. On this account Moses has given you circumcision (not because it is from Moses, but from the fathers); and on the Sabbath you circumcise a man. If a man receives circumcision on the Sabbath that the Law of Moses may not be broken, are you angry with Me because I made an entire man well on the Sabbath? Do not judge according to appearance, but judge with righteous judgment." Some of the people of Jerusalem were saying, "Is this not the man whom they are seeking to kill? And look, He is speaking publicly, and they are saying nothing to Him. The rulers do not really know that this is the Christ, do they? However we know where this man is from; but whenever the Christ may come, no one knows where He is from." Jesus therefore cried out in the temple, teaching and saying, "You both know Me, and know where I am from; and I have not come of Myself, but He who sent Me is true, whom you do not know. I know Him; because I am from Him, and He sent Me." They were seeking to seize Him; and no man laid his hand on Him, because His hour had not yet come. But many of the multitude believed in Him; and they were saying, "When the Christ shall come, He will not perform more signs than those which this man has, will He?" The Pharisees heard the multitude muttering these things about Him; and the chief priests and the Pharisees sent officers to seize Him. Jesus said, "For a little while longer I am with you, then I go to Him who sent Me. You shall seek Me, and shall not find Me; and where I am, you cannot come." The Jews said to one another, "Where does this man intend to go that we shall not find Him? He is not intending to go to the dispersion among the Greeks, and teach the Greeks, is He? What is this statement that He said, 'You will seek Me, and will not find Me; and where I am, you cannot come?'"

Now on the last day, the great day of the feast, Jesus stood and cried out, saying, "If any man is thirsty, let him come to Me and drink. He who believes in Me, as the Scripture said, 'From his innermost being shall flow rivers of living water.'" But this He spoke of the Spirit, whom those who believed in Him were to receive; for the Spirit was no yet given, because Jesus was not yet glorified. Some of the multitude, when they heard these words, were saying, "This certainly is the Prophet." Others were saying, "This is the Christ." Still others were saying, "Surely the Christ is not going to come from Galilee, is He? Has not the Scripture said that the Christ comes from of David, and from Bethlehem, the village where David was?" So there arose a division in the multitude because of Him. Some of them wanted to seize Him, but no one laid hands on Him. The officers came to the chief priests and Pharisees, and they said to them, "Why did you no bring Him?" The officers answered, "Never did a man speak the way this man speaks." The Pharisees answered them, "You have not also been led astray, have you? No one of the rulers or Pharisees has believed in Him has he? But this multitude which does not know the Law is accursed." Nicodemus said to them (he who came to Him before, being on of them), "Our Law does not judge a man, unless if first hears from him and knows what his is doing, does it?" They answered and said to him, "You are not also from Galilee, are you? Search, and see that no prophet arises out of Galilee." And everyone went to his home.

CHAPTER THIRTY ONE

Jesus went to the Mount of Olives. Early in the morning He came again into the temple, and all the people were coming to Him; and He sat down and began to teach them. The scribes and the Pharisees brought a woman caught in adultery, and having set her in the midst, they said to Him, "Teacher, this woman has been caught in adultery, in the very act. Now in the Law, Moses commanded us to stone such women; what then do You say?" They were saying this, testing Him, in order that they might have grounds for accusing Him. But Jesus stooped down, and with His finger wrote on the ground. When they persisted in asking Him, He straightened up, and said, to them, "He who is without sin among you, let him be the first to throw a stone at her." Again He stopped down, and wrote on the ground. When they heard it, they began to go out one by one, beginning with the older ones, and He was left alone, and the woman, where she had been, in the midst. Straightening up, Jesus said to her, "Woman, where are they? Did no one condemn you?" She said, "No one, Lord." And Jesus said, "Neither do I condemn you; go your way; from now on sin no more."

Jesus starting speaking again, and spoke saying, "I am the light of the world; he who follows Me shall not walk in the darkness, but shall have the light of life." The Pharisees therefore said to Him, "You are bearing witness of Yourself; Your witness is not true." Jesus answered and said to them, "Even if I bear witness of Myself, My witness is true; for I know where I came from, and where I am going; but you do not know where I come from, or where I am going. You people judge according to the flesh; I am not judging any one. But even if I do judge,

My judgment is true; for I am not alone in it, but I and He who sent Me. Even in your law it has been written, that the testimony of two men is true. I am He who bears witness of Myself, and the Father who sent Me bears witness of Me." These words He spoke in the treasury, as He taught in the temple; and no one seized Him, because His hour had not yet come. He said again to them, "I go away, and you shall seek Me, and shall die in your sin; where I am going, you cannot come." Therefore the Jews were saying, "Surely He will not kill Himself, will He, since He said, "Where I am going, you cannot come?" He was saying to them, "You are from below, I am from above; you are of this world; I am not of this world. I said to you, that you shall die in your sins; for unless you believe that I am He, you shall die in your sins." They were saying to Him, "Who are You?" Jesus said to them, "What have I been saying to you from the beginning? I have many things to speak and to judge concerning you, but He who sent Me is true; and the things which I heard from Him, these I speak to the world." They did not realize that He had been speaking to them about the Father. Jesus said, "When you lift up the Son of Man, then you will know that I am He, and I do nothing on My own initiative, but I speak these things as the Father taught Me. And He who sent Me is with Me; He has not left Me alone, for I always do the things that are pleasing to Him." As He spoke these things, many came to believe in Him. Jesus was saying to those Jews who had believed Him, "If you abide in My word, then you are truly disciples of Mine: and you shall know the truth, and the truth shall make you free." They answered Him, "We are Abraham's offspring, and have never yet been enslaved to anyone; how is it that You say, 'You shall become free?'" Jesus answered them, "Truly, truly, I say to you, every one who commits sin is the slave of sin. And the slave does not remain in the house forever; the Son does remain forever. If the Son shall make you free, you shall be free indeed. I know that you are Abraham's offspring; yet you seek to kill Me, because My word has no place in you. I speak the things which I have seen with My Father; therefore you also do the things which you heard from your father." They answered and said to Him, "Abraham is our father." Jesus said to them, "If you are Abraham's children, do the deeds of Abraham. But as it is, you are;

seeking to kill Me, a man who has told you the truth, which I heard from God; this Abraham did not do. You are doing the deeds of your father." They said to Him, "We were not born of fornication; we have a Father, even God." Jesus said to them, "If God were your Father, you would love Me; for I proceeded forth and have come from God, for I have not even come on My own initiative, but He sent Me. Why do you not understand what I am saying? It is because you cannot hear My word. You are of your father the devil, and you want to do the desires of your father. He was a murderer from the beginning, and does not stand in the truth, because there is no truth in him. Whenever he speaks a lie, he speaks from his own nature; for he is a liar, and the father of lies. But because I speak the truth, you do not believe Me. Which one of you convicts Me of sin? If I speak truth, why do you not believe Me? He who is of God hears the words of God; for this reason you do not hear them, because you are not of God." The Jews answered and said to Him, "Do we not say rightly that You are a Samaritan and have a demon?" Jesus answered, "I do not have a demon; but I honor My Father, and you dishonor Me. But I do not seek My glory; there is One who seeks and judges. Truly, truly, I say to you if anyone keeps My word he shall never see death." The Jews said to Him, "Now we know that You have a demon. Abraham died, and the prophets also; and You say, 'If anyone keeps My word, he shall never taste of death.' Surely You are not greater than our father Abraham, who died? The prophets died too; whom do You make Yourself out to be?" Jesus answered, "If I glorify Myself, My glory is nothing; it is My Father who glorifies Me, of whom you say, 'He is our God'; and you have not come to know Him, but I know Him; and if I say that I do not know Him, I shall be a liar like you, but I do know Him, and keep His word. Your father Abraham rejoiced to see My day; and he saw it, and was glad." The Jews therefore said to Him, "You are not yet fifty years old, and have You seen Abraham?" Jesus said to them, "Truly, truly, I say to you, before Abraham was born, I AM." Therefore they picked up stones to throw at Him; but Jesus hid Himself, and went out the temple.

CHAPTER THIRTY TWO

A certain lawyer stood up and put Him to the test, saying, "Teacher, what shall I do to inherit eternal life?" He said to him, "What is written in the Law? How does it read to you?" He answered and said, "You shall love the Lord you God with all your heart, and with all your soul, and with all your strength, and with all your mind; and your neighbor as your self." He said to him, "You have answered correctly; do this, and you will live." Wishing to justify himself, he said to Jesus, "And who is my neighbor?" Jesus replied and said, "A certain man was going down from Jerusalem to Jericho; and he fell among robbers, and they stripped him and beat him, and went off leaving him half dead. By chance a certain priest was going down on that road, and when he saw him, he passed by on the other side. And likewise a Levite also, when he came to the place and saw him, passed by on the other side. But a certain Samaritan, who was on a journey, came upon him; and when he saw him, he felt compassion, came to him, and bandaged up his wounds, pouring oil and wine on them; and he put him on his own beast, and brought him to an inn, and took care of him. On the next day he took out two denarii and gave them to the innkeeper and said, 'Take care of him; and whatever more you spend, when I return, I will repay you.' Which of these three do you think proved to be a neighbor to the man who fell into the robber's hands?" he said, "The one who showed mercy toward him." Jesus said to him, "Go and do the same."

Now as they were traveling along, He entered a certain village; and a woman named Martha welcomed Him into her home. She had a sister called Mary, who moreover was listening to the Lord's word seated at His feet. But Martha was distracted with all her preparations; and she came up to Him, and said, "Lord, do You not care that my sister has left me to do all the serving alone? Tell her to help me." But the lord answered and said to her, "Martha, Martha, you are worried and bothered about so many things; but only a few things are necessary, really only one, for Mary has chosen the good part, which shall not be taken away from her."

Jesus was speaking again to them, "Suppose one of you shall have a friend, and shall go to him at midnight, and say to him, 'Friend, lend me three loaves; for a friend of mine has come to me from a journey, and I have nothing to set before him;' and from inside he shall answer and say, 'Do not bother me; the door has already been shut and my children and I are in bed; I cannot get up and give you anything.' I tell you, even though he will not get up and give you anything because he is your friend, yet because of your persistence he will get up and give you as much as you need. I say to you, ask and it shall be given to you; seek, and you shall find; knock, and it shall be opened to you. For everyone who asks, receives; and he who seeks, finds; and to him who knocks, it shall be opened. Now suppose one of you fathers is asked by his son for a fish; he will not give him a snake instead of a fish, will he? Or if he is asked for an egg, he will not give him a scorpion, will he? If you then, being evil, know how to give good gifts to your children, how much more shall your heavenly Father give the Holy Spirit to those who ask Him?"

CHAPTER THIRTY THREE

The seventy He sent out returned with joy, saying, "Lord, even the demons are subject to us in Your name." He said to them, "I was watching Satan fall from heaven like lightning. Behold, I have given you authority to tread upon serpents and scorpions, and over all the power of the enemy, and nothing shall injure you. Nevertheless do not rejoice in this, that the spirits are subject to you, but rejoice that your names are recorded in heaven."

At that very time He rejoiced greatly in the Holy Spirit, and said, "I praise Thee, O Father, Lord of heaven and earth, that Thou didst hide these things from the wise and intelligent and didst reveal them to babes. Yes, Father, for thus it was well pleasing in Thy sight. All things have been handed over to Me by My Father, and no one knows who the Son is except the Father, and who the Father is except the Son, and anyone to whom the Son wills to reveal Him."

CHAPTER THIRTY FOUR

As He passed by, He saw a man blind from birth. His disciples asked Him, saying, "Rabbi, who sinned, this man or his parents, that he should be born blind?" Jesus answered, "It was neither that this man sinned, nor his parents; but it was in order that the works of God might be displayed in him. We must work the works of Him who sent Me, as long as it is day; night is coming, when no man can work. While I am in the world, I am the light of the world." When He had said this, he spat on the ground, and made clay of the spittle, and applied the clay to his eyes, and said to him, "Go, wash in the pool of Siloam" (which is translated, Sent). So he went away and washed, and came back seeing. The neighbors, and those who previously saw him as a beggar, were saying, "Is not this the one who used to sit and beg?" Others were saying, "This is he," still others were saying, "No, but he is like him." He kept saying, "I am the one." They were saying to him, "How then were your eyes opened?" He answered, "The man who is called Jesus made clay, and anointed my eyes, and said to me, 'Go to Siloam, and wash'; so I went away and washed, and I received sight." They said to him, "Where is He?" He said, "I do not know." They brought to the Pharisees him who was formerly blind. Now it was a Sabbath on the day when Jesus made the clay, and opened his eyes. Again, the Pharisees also were asking him how he received his sight. He said to them, "He applied clay to my eyes, and I washed, and I see." Some of Pharisees were saying, "This man is not from God, because He does not keep the Sabbath." But others were saying "How can a man who is a sinner perform such signs?" There was a division among them.

They said to the blind man again, "What do you say about Him since He opened your eyes?" And he said, "He is a prophet." The Jews did not believe it of him, that he had been blind, and had received sight, until they called the parents of the very one who had received his sight, and questioned them, saying, "Is this your son, who you say was born blind? Then how does he now see?" His parents answered them and said, "We know that this is our son, and that he was born blind; but how he now sees, we do not know; or who opened his eyes, we do not know. Ask him; he is of age, he shall speak for himself." His parents said this because they were afraid of the Jews; for the Jews had already agreed, that if any one should confess Him to be Christ, he should be put out of the synagogue. For this reason his parents said, "He is of age; ask him." So a second time they called the man who had been blind, and said to him, "Give glory to God; we know that this man is a sinner." He answered, "Whether He is a sinner, I do not know; one thing I do know, that, whereas I was blind, now I see." They said to him, "What did He do to you? How did He open your eyes?" He answered them, "I told you already, and you did not listen; why do you want to hear it again? You do not want to become His disciples too, do you?" They reviled him, and said, "You are His disciple; but we are disciples of Moses. We know that God has spoken to Moses; but as for this man, we do not know where He is from." The man answered and said to them, "Well, here is an amazing thing, that you do not know where He is from, and yet He opened my eyes. We know that God does not hear sinners: but if any one is God fearing, and does His will, He hears him. Since the beginning of time it has never been heard that any one opened the eyes of a person born blind. If this man were not from God, He could do nothing." They answered and said to him, "You were born entirely in sin, and are you teaching us?" They put him out. Jesus heard that they had put him out; and finding him, He said, "Do you believe in the Son of Man?" He answered and said, "Who is He, Lord, that I may believe in Him?" Jesus said to him, "You have both seen Him, and He is the one who is talking with you." He said, "Lord, I believe." And he worshiped Him. Jesus said, "For judgment I came into world, that those who do not see may see; and that those who see may become blind." Those of the Pharisees who were with Him heard these things, and said to Him, "We are not blind too, are we?" Jesus said to them, "If you were blind, you would have no sin, but now you say, 'We see; your sin remains.'"

Chapter Thirty Five

"Truly, Truly, I say to you, he who does not enter by the door into the fold of the sheep, but climbs up some other way, he is a thief and a robber. But he who enters by the door is a shepherd of the sheep. To him the doorkeeper opens, and the sheep hear his voice, and he calls his own sheep by name, and leads them out. When he puts forth all his own, he goes before them, and the sheep follow him because they know his voice. A stranger they simply will not follow, but will flee from him, because they do not know the voice of strangers." This figure of speech Jesus spoke to them, but they did not understand what those things were which He had been saying to them. Jesus said to them again, "Truly, truly, I say to you, I am the door of the sheep. All who came before Me are thieves and robbers; but the sheep did not hear them. I am the door; if anyone enters through Me, he shall be saved, and shall go in and out, and find pasture. The thief comes only to steal, and kill, and destroy; I came that they might have life, and might have it abundantly. I am the good shepherd; the good shepherd lays down His life for the sheep. He who is a hireling, and not a shepherd, who is not the owner of the sheep, beholds the wolf coming, and leaves the sheep, and flees, and the wolf snatches them, and scatters them. He flees because he is a hireling, and is not concerned about the sheep. I am the good shepherd; and I know My own, and My own know Me, even as the Father knows Me and I know the Father; and I lay down My life for the sheep. And I have other sheep, which are not of the fold; I must bring them also, and they shall hear My voice; and they shall become one flock with one shepherd. For this reason the Father loves Me, because I lay down My life that I may take it again. No one has taken it away from Me, but I lay it down on My own initiative. I have authority to lay it down, and I have authority to take it up again. This commandment I received from My Father." There arose a division again among the Jews because of these words. Many of them were saying "He has a demon, and is insane; why so you listen to Him?" Others were saying, "These are not the sayings of one demon possessed. A demon cannot open the eyes of the blind, can he?" At that time the Feast of the Dedication took place at Jerusalem; it was winter, and Jesus was walking in the temple in the portico of Solomon. The Jews gathered around Him, and were saying to Him, "How long will You keep us in suspense? If You are the Christ, tell us plainly." Jesus answered them, "I told you, and you do not believe; the works that I do in My Father's name, these bear witness of Me. But you do not believe, because you are not of My sheep. My sheep hear My voice, and I know them, and they follow Me; and I give eternal life to them, and they shall never perish; and no one shall snatch them out of My hand. My Father, who has given them to Me, is greater than all; and no one is able to snatch them out the Father's hand. I and the Father are one."

The Jews took up stones again to stone Him. Jesus answered them, "I showed you many good works from the Father; for which of them are you stoning Me?" The Jews answered Him, "For a good work we do not stone You, but for blasphemy; and because You, being a man, make Yourself out to be God." Jesus answered them, "Has it not been written in your Law, 'I said, you are gods'? If He called them gods, to whom the word of God came (and the Scripture cannot be broken), do you say to Him, whom the Father sanctified and sent into the world, 'You are blaspheming,' because I said, 'I am the Son of God'? If I do not do the works of My Father, do not believe Me; but if I do them, though you do not believe Me, believe the works, that you may know and understand that the Father is in Me, and I in the Father." They were seeking again to seize Him; and He eluded their grasp. He went away again beyond the Jordan to the place where John was first baptizing; and He was staying there. Many came to Him; and they were saying, "While John performed no sign, yet everything John said about this man was true." Many believed in Him there.

CHAPTER THIRTY SIX

Now a certain man was sick, Lazarus of Bethany, of the village of Mary and her sister Martha. It was the Mary who anointed the Lord with ointment, and wiped His feet with her hair, whose brother Lazarus was sick. The sisters went to Him, saying, "Lord, behold, he whom You love is sick." But when Jesus heard it, He said, "This sickness is not unto death, but for the glory of God, that the Son of God may be glorified by it." Now Jesus loved Martha, her sister, and Lazarus. When He heard that he was sick, He stayed there two days longer in the place where He was. Then after this He said to the disciples, "Let us go to Judea again." The disciples said to Him, "Rabbi, the Jews were just now seeking to stone You; and are You going there again?" Jesus answered, "Are there not twelve hours in the day? If anyone walks in the day, he does not stumble, because he sees the light of the world. But if anyone walks in the night, he stumbles, because the light is not in him." This He said, and after that He said to them, "Our friend Lazarus has fallen asleep; but I go, that I may awaken him out of sleep." The disciples said to Him, "Lord, if he has fallen asleep, he will recover." Now Jesus had spoken of his death; but they thought that He speaking of literal sleep. Then Jesus said to them plainly, "Lazarus is dead, and I am glad for your sakes that I was not there, so that you may believe; but let us go to him." Thomas, who is called Didymus, said to his fellow disciples, "Let us also go, that we may die with him." So when Jesus came, he found that he had already been in the tomb four days. Now Bethany was near Jerusalem, about two miles off; and many of the Jews had come to Martha and Mary, to console them concerning their brother. Martha, when she heard that Jesus was coming, went to meet Him; but Mary still sat in the house. Martha said to Jesus, "Lord, if You had been here, my brother would not have died. Even now I know that whatever You ask of God, God will give You." Jesus said to her, "Your brother shall rise again." Martha said to Him "I know that he will rise again in the resurrection on the last day." Jesus said to her, "I am the resurrection and life; he who believes in Me shall live even if he dies. Do you believe this?" She said to Him, "Yes, Lord; I have believed that You are the Christ, the Son of God, even He who comes into the world." When she had said this, she went away, and called Mary her sister, saying secretly, "The Teacher is here, and is calling for you." When she heard it, she arose quickly, and was coming to Him. Now Jesus had not yet come into the village, but was still in the place where Martha met Him. The Jews then who were with her in the house, and consoling her, when they saw that Mary rose up quickly and went out, followed her, supposing that she was going to the tomb to weep there. When Mary came where Jesus was, she saw Him, and fell at His feet, saying to Him, "Lord, if You had been here, my brother would not have died." When Jesus saw her weeping, and the Jews who came with her, also weeping, He was deeply moved in spirit, and was troubled, and said, "Where have you laid him?" They said to Him, "Lord, come and see." Jesus wept. So the Jews were saying, "Behold how He loved him!" But some of them said, "Could not this man, who opened the eyes of him who was blind, have kept this man also from dying?" Jesus therefore again being deeply moved within, came to the tomb. Now it was a cave, and a stone was lying against it. Jesus said, "Remove the stone." Martha, the sister of the deceased, said to Him, "Lord, by this time there will be a stench; for he has been dead four days." Jesus said to her, "Did I not say to you, if you believe, you will see the glory of God?" So they removed the stone. Jesus raised His eyes, and said, "Father, I thank Thee that Thou heardest Me. And I knew that Thou hearest Me always; but because of the people standing around I said it, that they may believe that Thou didst send Me." When He had said these things, He cried out with a loud voice, "Lazarus, come forth." He who had died came forth, bound hand and foot with wrappings; and his face was wrapped around with a cloth, Jesus said to them, "Unbind him, and let him go."

Many of the Jews, who had come to Mary and behold what He had done, believed in Him. But some of them went away to the Pharisees, and told them the things which Jesus had done. The chief priests and the Pharisees convened a council, and were saying, "What are we doing? For this man is performing many signs. If we let Him go on like this, all men will believe in Him, and the Romans will come and take away both our place and our nation." But a certain one of them, Caiaphas, who was high priest that year, said to them, "You know nothing at all, nor do you take into account that it is expedient for you that one man should die for the people, and that the whole nation should not perish." Now this he did not say on his own initiative; but being high priest that year, he prophesied that Jesus was going to die for the nation; and not for the nation only, but that He might also gather together into one the children of God who are scattered abroad. So from that day on they planned together to kill Him. Jesus therefore no longer continued to walk publicly among the Jews, but went away from there to the country near the wilderness, into a city called Ephraim; and there He stayed with the disciples. Now the Passover of the Jews was at hand, and many went up to Jerusalem out of the country before the Passover, to purify themselves. They were seeking Jesus, and were saying to one another, as they stood in the temple, "What do you think; that He will not come to the feast at all?" Now the chief priests and the Pharisees had given orders that if any one knew where He was, he should report it, that they might seize Him.

Rising up, He went from there to the region of Judea, and beyond the Jordan; and crowds gathered around Him again, and according to His custom, He once more began to teach them. The great multitudes followed Him, and He healed them.

Now on this occasion there were some present who reported to Him about the Galileans, whose blood Pilate had mingled with their sacrifices. He answered and said to them, "Do you suppose that these Galileans were greater sinners than all other Galileans, because they suffered this fate? I tell you, no but, unless you repent, you will all likewise perish. Or do you suppose that those eighteen on whom the tower in Siloam fell and killed them, were worse culprits than all the men who live in Jerusalem? I tell you, no, but, unless you repent, you will all likewise perish."

CHAPTER THIRTY SEVEN

He was teaching in one of the synagogues on the Sabbath. And behold, there was a woman who for eighteen years had had a sickness caused by a spirit; and she was bent double, and could not straighten up at all. When Jesus saw her, He called her over and said to her, "Woman, you are freed from your sickness." He laid His hands upon her; and immediately she was made erect again, and began glorifying God. The synagogue official, indignant because Jesus had healed on the Sabbath, began saying to the multitude in response, "There are six days in which work should be done; therefore come during them and get healed, and not on the Sabbath day." But the Lord answered him and said, "You hypocrites, does not each of you on the Sabbath untie his ox or his donkey from the stall, and lead him away to water him? And this woman, a daughter of Abraham as she is, whom Satan had bound for eighteen long years, should she not have been released from this bond on the Sabbath day?" As He said this, all His opponents were being humiliated; and the entire multitude was rejoicing over all the glorious things being done by Him.

Someone said to Him, "Lord, are there just a few who are being saved?" And He said to them, "Strive to enter by the narrow door; for many, I tell you, will seek to enter and will not be able. Once the head of the house gets up and shuts the door, and you begin to stand outside and knock on the door, saying, 'Lord, open up to us!' then He will answer and say, to you, 'I do not know where you are from.' Then you will begin to say, 'We ate and drank in Your presence, and You taught in our streets'; and He will say, 'I tell you, I do not know where you are from; depart from Me, all you evildoers.' There will be weeping and gnashing of teeth there when you see Abraham and Isaac and Jacob and all the prophets in the kingdom of God, but yourselves being cast out. They will come from east and west, from north and south, and will recline at table in the kingdom of God. And behold, some are last who will be first and some are first who will be last."

Just at that time some Pharisees came up, saying to Him, "Go away and depart from here, for Herod wants to kill you." He said to them, "Go and tell that fox, 'Behold, I cast out demons and perform cures today and tomorrow, and the third day I reach My goal.' Nevertheless I must journey on today and tomorrow and the next day; for it cannot be that a prophet should perish outside of Jerusalem. O Jerusalem, Jerusalem, the city that kills the prophets and stones those sent to her! How often I wanted to gather your children together, just as a hen gathers her brood under her wings, and you would not have it! Behold, your house is left to you desolate; and I say to you, you shall not see Me until the time comes when you say, 'Blessed is He who comes in the name of the Lord!'"

Chapter Thirty Eight

I t came about when He went into the house of one of the leaders of the Pharisees on the Sabbath to eat bread, that they were watching Him closely. There, in front of Him was a certain man suffering from dropsy. Jesus answered and spoke to the lawyers and Pharisees, saying, "Is it lawful to heal on the Sabbath, or not?" They kept silent. He took hold of him, and healed him, and sent him away. He said to them, "Which one of you shall have a son or an ox fall into a well, and will not immediately pull him out on a Sabbath day?" They could make no reply to this.

He began speaking a parable to the invited guests when He noticed how they had been picking out the places of honor at the table; saying to them, "When you are invited by someone to a wedding feast, do not take the place of honor, lest someone more distinguished than you may have been invited by him, and he who invited you both shall come and say to you, 'Give place to this man', and then in disgrace you proceed to occupy the last place. But when you are invited, go and recline at the last place, so that when the one who has invited you comes, he may say to you, 'Friend, move up higher'; then you will have honor in the sight of all who are at the table with you. For everyone who exalts himself shall be humbled, and he who humble himself shall be exalted." He also went on to say to the one who had invited Him, "When you give a luncheon or a dinner, do not invite your friends or your brothers or your relatives or rich neighbors, lest they also invite you in return, and repayment come to you. But when you give a reception, invite the poor, the crippled, the lame, the blind, and you will be blessed, since they do not have the means to repay you; for you will be repaid at the resurrection of the righteous." One of those who were reclining at table with Him heard this, he said to Him, "Blessed is everyone who shall eat bread in the kingdom of God!" But He said to him, "A certain man was giving a big dinner, and he invited many; and at the dinner hour he sent his slave to say to those who had been invited, 'Come, for everything is ready now.' But they all alike began to make excuses. The first one said to him, 'I have bought a piece of land and I need to go out and look at it; please consider me excused.' And another one said, 'I have bought five yoke of oxen, and I am going to try them out; please consider me excused.' And another one said, "I have married a wife, and for that reason I cannot come.' The slave came back and reported this to his master. Then the head of the household became angry and said to his slave. 'Go out at once into the streets and lanes of the city and bring in here the poor and crippled and blind and lame.' And the slave said, 'Master, what you commanded has been done, and still there is room.' And the master said to the slave, 'Go out into the highways and along the hedges, and compel them to come in, that my house may be filled. For I tell you, none of those men who were invited shall taste of my dinner.'"

CHAPTER THIRTY NINE

N ow great multitudes were going along with Him; and He turned and said to them, "If anyone come to Me, and does not hate his own father and mother and wife and children and brothers and sisters, yes, and even his own life, he cannot be My disciple. Whoever does not carry his own cross and come after Me cannot be My disciple. For which one of you, when he wants to build a tower, does not first sit down and calculate the cost, to see if he has enough to complete it? Otherwise, when he has laid a foundation, and is not able to finish, all who observe it begin to ridicule him, saying 'This man began to build and was not able to finish.' Or what king, when he sets out to meet another king in battle, will not first sit down and counsel whether he is strong enough with ten thousand men to encounter the one coming against him with twenty thousand? Or else, while the other is still far away, he sends a delegation and asks terms of peace. So therefore, no one of you can be My disciple who does not give up all his own possessions."

Now all the tax gathers and the sinners were coming near Him to listen to Him. Both the Pharisees and the scribes began to grumble, saying, "This man receives sinners and eats with them." He told them this parable, saying, "What man among you, if he has a hundred sheep, and has lost one of them, does not leave the ninety nine in the open pasture, and go after the one which is lost, until he finds it? And when he has found it, he lays it on his shoulders, rejoicing. When he comes home, he calls together his friends and his neighbors, saying to them, 'Rejoice with me, for I have found my sheep which was lost!' I tell you that in the same way, there will be more joy in heaven over one sinner who repents, than over ninety nine righteous persons who need no repentance. Or what woman, if she has ten silver coins and lose one coin, does not light a lamp and sweep the house and search carefully until she finds it? And when she has found it, she calls together her friends and neighbors, saying, 'Rejoice with me, for I have found the coin which I had lost!' In the same way, I tell you, there is joy in the presence of the angels of God over one sinner who repents."

And He said, "A certain man had two sons; and the younger of them said to his father, 'Father, give me the share of the estate that falls to me.' And he divided his wealth between them. Not many days later, the younger son gathered everything together and went on a journey into a distant country, and there he squandered his estate with loose living. Now he had spent everything, a severe famine occurred in that country, and he began to be in need. He went and attached himself to one of the citizens of that country, and he sent him into his fields to feed swine. He was longing to fill his stomach with the pods that the swine were eating, and no one was giving anything to him. When he came to his senses, he said, 'How many of my father's hired men have more than enough bread, but I am dying here with hunger! I will get up and go to my father, and will say to him, "Father, I have sinned against heaven, and in your sight; I am no longer worthy to be called your son; make me as one of your hired men." He got up and came to his father. But while he was still a long way off, his father saw him, and felt compassion for him, and ran and embraced him, and kissed him. The son said to him, 'Father, I have sinned against heaven and in your sight; I am no longer worthy to be called your son.' But the father said to his slaves, 'Quickly bring out the best robe and put it on him, and put a ring on his hand and sandals on his feet; and bring the fattened calf, kill it, and let us eat and be merry; for this son of mine was dead, and has come to life again; he was lost, and has been found.' And they began to be merry. Now his older son was in the field, and when he came and approached the house, he heard music and dancing. He summoned one of the servants and began inquiring what these things might be. He said to him, 'Your brother has come home, and your father has killed the fattened calf, because he has received him back safe and sound.' But he became angry, and was not willing to go in; and his father came out and began entreating him. But he answered and said to his father, 'Look! For so many years I have been serving you, and I have never neglected a command of yours; and yet you have never given me a calf, that I might be merry with my friends; but when this son of yours came, who has devoured your wealth with harlots, you killed the fattened calf for him.' And he said to him, 'My child, you have always been with me, and all that is mine is yours. But we had to be merry and rejoice, for this brother of yours was dead and has begun to live, and was lost and has been found.'"

Chapter Forty

N ow He was also saying to the disciples, "There was a certain rich man who had a steward, and this steward was reported to him as squandering his possessions. He called him and said to him, 'What is this I hear about you? Give an account of your stewardship, for you can no longer be steward.' The steward said to himself, 'What shall I do, since my master is taking the stewardship away from me? I am not strong enough to dig; I am ashamed to beg. I know what I shall do, so that when I am removed from the stewardship, they will receive me into their home.' He summoned each one of his master's debtors, and he began saying to the first, 'How much do you owe my master?' And he said, 'A hundred measures of oil.' And he said to him, 'Take you bill, and sit down quickly and write fifty.' Then he said to another, 'And how much do you owe?' And he said, 'A hundred measures of wheat.' He said to him, 'Take your bill, and write eighty.' His master praised the unrighteous steward because he had acted shrewdly; for the sons of this age are more shrewd in relation to their own kind than the sons of light. I say to you, make friends for yourselves by means of the mammon of unrighteousness; that when it fails, they may receive you into the eternal dwellings. He who is faithful in a very little thing is faithful also in much; and he who is unrighteous in a very little thing is unrighteous also in much. If you have not been faithful in the use of unrighteous mammon, who will entrust the true riches to you? And if you have not been faithful in the use of that which is another's, who will give you that which is your own? No servant can serve two masters; for either he will hate the one, and love the other, or else he will hold to one, and despise the other. You cannot serve God and mammon."

Now the Pharisees, who were lovers of money, were listening to all these things, and they were scoffing at Him. He said to them, "You are those who justify yourselves in the sight of men, but God knows your hearts; for that which is highly esteemed a among men is detestable in the sight of God. The law and the Prophets were proclaimed until John; since then the gospel of the kingdom of God is preached, and every one is forcing his way into it. But it is easier for heaven and earth to pass away than for one stroke of a letter of Law to fail. Now there was a certain rich man, and he habitually dressed in purple and fine linen, gaily living in splendor every day. A certain poor man named Lazarus was laid at his gate, covered with sores, and longing to be fed with the crumbs which were falling from the rich man's table; besides even the dogs were coming and licking his sores. Now it came about that the poor man died and he was carried away by the angels to Abraham's bosom; and the rich man also died and was buried. And in Hades he lifted up his eyes, being to torment, and saw Abraham far away, and Lazarus in his bosom. And he cried out and said, 'Father Abraham have mercy on me, and send Lazarus, that he may dip the tip of his finger in water and cool off my tongue; for I am in agony in this flame.' But Abraham said, 'Child remember that during your life you received your good things, and likewise Lazarus had things; but now he is being comforted here, and you are in agony. And besides all this, between us and you there is a great chasm fixed, in order that those who wish to come over from here to you may not be able, and that none may cross over from there to us.' And he said, 'Then I beg you, Father, that you send him to my father's house, for I have five brothers, that he may warn them, lest they also come to this place to torment.' But Abraham said, 'They have Moses and the Prophets; let them hear them.' But he said, "No, Father Abraham, but if someone goes to them from the dead, they will repent!' But he said to him, 'If they do not listen to Moses and the Prophets, neither will they be persuaded if someone rise from the dead.'"

CHAPTER FORTY ONE

He said to His disciples, "It is inevitable that stumbling blocks should come, but woe to him through whom they come! It would be better for him if a millstone were hung around his neck and he were thrown into the sea, that he should cause one of these little ones to stumble. Be on your guard! If your brother sins, rebuke him; and if he repents, forgive him. And if he sins against you seven times a day, and returns to you seven times, saying, 'I repent,' forgive him.'"

The apostles said to the Lord, "Increase our faith!" The Lord said, "If you had faith like a mustard seed, you would say to this mulberry tree, 'Be uprooted and be planted in the sea'; and it would obey you. But which of you, having a slave plowing or tending sheep, will say to him when he has come in from the field, 'Come immediately and sit down to eat'? But will he not say to him?, 'Prepare something for me until I have eaten and drunk; and afterward you will eat and drink?' He does not thank the slave because he did the things which were commanded, does he? So you too, when you do all the things which are commanded you, say, 'We are unworthy slaves; we have done only that which we ought to have done.'"

Now having been questioned by the Pharisees as to when the kingdom of God was coming. He answered them and said, "The kingdom of God is not coming with signs to be observed; nor will they say, 'Look, here it is!' or, 'There it is!' For behold, the kingdom of God is in your midst." He said to the disciples, "The days shall come when you will long to see one of the days of the Son of Man, and you will not see it. And they will say to you, 'Look there! Look here!' Do not go away, and do not run after them. For just as the lightning, when it flashes out of one part of the sky, shines to the other part of the sky, so will the Son of Man be in His day. But first He must suffer many things and be rejected by this generation. And just as it happened in the days of Noah, so it shall be also in the days on the Son of Man; they were eating, they were drinking, they were marrying, they were being given in marriage, until the day that Noah entered the ark, and the flood came and destroyed them all. It was the same as happened in the days of Lot; they were eating, they were drinking, they were buying, they were selling, they were planting, they were building; but on the day that Lot went out from Sodom it rained fire and brimstone from heaven and destroyed them all. It will be just the same on the day that the Son of Man is revealed. On that day, let not the one who is on the housetop and whose goods are in the house go down to take them away; and likewise let not the one who is in the field turn back. Remember Lot's wife. Whoever seeks to keep his life shall lose it, and whoever loses his life shall preserve it alive. I tell you, on that night there will be two in one bed; one will be taken, and the other will be left. There will be two women grinding at the same place; one will be taken, and the other will be left. Two men will be in the field; one will be taken and the other will be left." Answering they said to Him, "Where, Lord?" He said to them, "Where the body is there also will the vultures be gathered."

Now He was telling them a parable to show that at all times they ought to pray and not to lose heart, saying, "There was in a certain city a judge who did not fear God, and did not respect man. There was a widow in the city, and she kept coming to him, saying, 'Give me legal protection from my opponent.' And for a while he was unwilling; but afterward he said to himself, 'Even though I do not fear God nor respect man, yet because this widow bothers me, I will give her legal protection, lest by continually coming she wear me out.'" The Lord said, "Hear what the unrighteous judge said; shall no God bring about justice for His elect, who cry to Him day and night, and will He delay long over them? I tell you that He will bring about justice for them speedily. However, when the Son of Man comes, will He find faith on the earth?"

He also told this parable to certain ones who trusted in themselves that they were righteous, and viewed others with contempt; "Two men went up into the temple to pray, one a Pharisee, and the other a tax gatherer. The Pharisee stood and was praying thus to himself, 'God, I thank Thee that I am not like other people; swindlers, unjust, adulterer, or even like this tax gatherer. I fast twice a week; I pay tithes of all that I get.' But the tax gatherer, standing some distance away, was even unwilling to lift up his eyes to heaven, but was beating his breast, saying, 'God, be merciful to me, the sinner!' I tell you, this man went down to his house justified rather than the other; for every one who exalts himself shall be humbled, but he who humbles himself shall be exalted."

CHAPTER FORTY TWO

Rising up, he went from there to the region of Judea, and beyond the Jordan; and crowds gathered around Him again, and according to His custom, he once more began to teach them. Some Pharisees came up to Him, testing Him, and began to question Him whether it was lawful for a man to divorce a wife. He answered and said to them, "What did Moses command you?" They said, "Moses permitted a man to write a certificate of divorce and send her away." But Jesus said to them, "Because of your hardness of heart he wrote you this commandment. But from the beginning of creation, God made them male and female. For this cause a man shall leave his father and mother, and the two shall became one flesh; consequently they are no longer two, but one flesh. What therefore God has joined together, let no man separate." In the house the disciples began questioning Him about this again. And He said to them, "Whoever divorces his wife and marries another woman commits adultery against her; and if she herself divorces her husband and marries another man, she is committing adultery." The disciples said to Him, "If the relationship of the man with his wife is like this, it is better not to marry." He said to them, "Not all men can accept this statement, but only those to whom it has been given. For there are eunuchs who were born that way from their mother's womb; and there are eunuchs who were made eunuchs by men; and there are also eunuchs who made themselves eunuchs for the sake of the kingdom of heaven. He who is able to accept this, let him accept it."

As He was setting out on a journey, a man ran up to Him and knelt before Him, and began asking Him, "Good Teacher, what shall I do to inherit eternal life?" Jesus said to him, "Why do you call Me good? No one is good except God alone. You know the commandments, 'Do not murder, Do not commit adultery, Do not steal, Do not bear false witness, Do not defraud, Honor your father, and mother.'" And he said to Him, "Teacher, I have kept all these things from my youth up." Looking at him, Jesus felt a love for him, and said to him, "One thing you lack; go and sell all you possess, and give it to the poor, and you shall have treasure in heaven; and come, follow Me." But at these words his face fell, and he went away grieved, for he was one who owned much property, and was very rich. Jesus, looking around, said to His disciples, "How hard it will be for those who are wealthy to enter the kingdom of God!" The disciples were amazed at His words. But Jesus answered again and said to them, "Children, how hard it is to enter the kingdom of God! It is easier for a camel to go through the eye of a needle than for a rich man to enter the kingdom of God." They were even more astonished and said to Him, "Then who can be saved?" Looking upon them, Jesus said, "With men it is impossible, but not with God; for all things are possible with God." Peter began to say to Him, "Behold, we have left everything and followed You." Jesus said, "Truly I say to you, there is no one who has left house or brothers or sisters or mother or father or children or farms, for My sake and for the gospel's sake, but that he shall receive a hundred times as much now in the present age, houses and brothers and sisters and mothers and children and farms, along with persecutions; and in the world to come, eternal life. But many who are first, will be last; and the last, first." Jesus said, "For the kingdom of heaven is like a landowner who went out early in the morning to hire laborers for his vineyard. And when he had agreed with the laborers for a denarius for the day, he sent them into his vineyard. And he went out about the third hour and saw others standing idle in the market place; and to those he said, 'You too go into the vineyard, and whatever is right I will give you.' And so they went. Again he went out about the sixth and the ninth hour, and did the same thing. About the eleventh hour he went out, and found others standing; and he said to them, 'Why have you been standing here idle all day long?' They said to him, 'Because no one hired us.' He said to them, 'You too go into the vineyard.' When evening had come, the owner of the vineyard said to his foreman, 'Call the laborers and pay them their wage, beginning with the last group to the first.' When those hired about the eleventh hour came, each one received a denarius. And when those hired first came, they thought that they would receive more; and they also received each one a denarius. When they received it, they grumbled at the landowner, saying, 'These last men have worked only one hour, and you have made them equal to us who have borne the burden and the scorching heat of the day.' But he answered and said to one of them, 'Friend, I am doing you no wrong; did you not agree with me for a denarius? Take what is yours and go your way, but I wish to give to this last man the same as to you. Is it not lawful for me to do what I wish with what is my own? Or is your eye envious because I am generous?' For the last shall be first, and the first last."

CHAPTER FORTY THREE

They were on the road, going up to Jerusalem, Jesus was walking on ahead of them; they were amazed, and those who followed were fearful. He took the twelve aside and began to tell them what was going to happen to Him, saying, "Behold, we are going up to Jerusalem, and all things which are written through the prophets about the Son of Man will be accomplished. For the Son of Man will be delivered up to the chief priests and the scribes; they will condemn Him to death, and will deliver Him up to the Gentiles. They will mock Him, spit upon Him, scourge Him, and kill Him, and three days later He will rise again." They understood none of these things, and this saying was hidden from them, and they did not comprehend the things that were said.

Then the Mother of James and John, the two sons of Zebedee, came up to Him, with her sons, bowing down, and making a request of Him. He said to her, "What do you wish?" She said to Him, "Command that in Your kingdom these two sons of mine may sit, one on Your right, and one on Your left." Jesus said to them, "You do not know what you are asking for. Are you able to drink the cup that I drink or to be baptized with the baptism with which I am baptized?" They said to Him, "We are able." Jesus said to them, "The cup that I drink you shall drink; and you shall be baptized with the baptism with which I am baptized. But to sit on My right or on My left, this is not Mine to give; but it is for those for whom it has been prepared." And hearing this, the ten began to feel indignant toward James and John. Calling them to Himself, Jesus said to them, "You know that those who are recognized as rulers of the Gentiles lord it over them; and their great men exercise authority over them. But it is not so among you, but whoever wishes to become great among you shall be your servant; and whoever wishes to be first among you shall be slave of all. For even the Son of Man did not come to be served, but to serve, and to give His life a ransom for many."

CHAPTER FORTY FOUR

I t came about that as He was approaching Jericho, a blind man named Bartimaeus, the son of Timaeus, was sitting by the road, begging. Now hearing a multitude going by, he began to inquire what this might be. They told him that Jesus of Nazareth was passing by. He called out, saying, "Jesus, Son of David, have mercy on me!" Those who led the way were sternly telling him to be quiet; but he kept crying out all the more, "Son of David, have mercy on me!" Jesus stopped and commanded that he be brought to Him. They called the blind man, saying to him, "Take courage, arise! He is calling for you." When he had come near, He questioned him, "What do you want Me to do for you?" He said, "Lord, I want to receive my sight!" Jesus said to him, "Receive your sight; your faith has made you well." Immediately he received his sight, and began following Him, glorifying God; and when all the people saw it, they gave praise to God.

He entered and was passing through Jericho. And behold, there was a man called by the name of Zaccheus; he was a chief tax gatherer, and he was rich. He was trying to see who Jesus was, and he was unable because of the crowd, for he was small in stature. He ran on ahead and climbed up into a sycamore tree in order to see Him, for He was about to pass through that way. When Jesus came to the place, He looked up and said to him, "Zaccheus, hurry and come down, for today I must stay at your house." He hurried and came down, and received Him gladly. When they saw it, they all began to grumble, saying, "He has gone to be the quest of a man who is a sinner." Zaccheus stopped and said to the Lord, "Behold, Lord, half of my possessions I will give to the poor, and if I have defrauded anyone of anything, I will give back four times as much." Jesus said to him, "Today salvation has come to this house, because he, too, is a son of Abraham. For the Son of Man has come to seek and to save that which was lost."

While they were listening to these things, He went on to tell a parable, because He was near Jerusalem, and they supposed that the kingdom of God was going to appear immediately. He said, "A certain nobleman went to a distant country to receive a kingdom for himself, and then return. He called ten of his slaves, and gave them ten minas, and said to them, 'Do business with this until I come back.' But his citizens hated him, and sent a delegation after him, saying, 'We do not want this man to reign over us.' And it came about that when he returned, after receiving the kingdom he ordered that these slaves, to whom he had given the money, be called to him in order that he might know what business they had done. The first appeared, saying, 'Master, your mina has made ten minas more.' And he said to him, 'Well done, good slave, because you have been faithful in a very little thing, be in authority over ten cities.' The second came, saying, 'Your mina, master, has made five minas.' And he said to him also, 'You are to be over five cities.' Another came, saying, 'Master, behold your mina, which I kept put away in a handkerchief; for I was afraid of you, because you are an exacting man; you take up what you did not lay down, and reap what you did not sow.' He said to him, 'By your own words I will judge you, you worthless slave. Did you know that I am an exacting man, taking up what I did not lay down, and reaping what I did not sow? Then why did you not put the money in the bank, and having come, I would have collected it with interest?' And he said to the bystander, 'Take the mina away from him, and give it to the one who has the ten minas.' They said to him, 'Master, he has ten minas already.' I tell you, that to everyone who has shall more be given, but from the one who does not have, even what he does have shall be taken away. But these enemies of mine, who did not want me to reign over them, bring them here, and slay them in my presence." After He had said these things, He was going on ahead, ascending to Jerusalem.

CHAPTER FORTY FIVE

Jesus, days before the Passover, said to His disciples, "You know that after two days the Passover is coming, and the Son of Man is to be delivered up for crucifixion." He came to Bethany where Lazarus was, whom Jesus had raised from the dead. So they made Him a supper there; and Martha was serving; but Lazarus was one of those reclining at the table with Him. Mary took a pound of very costly, genuine spikenard ointment, and anointed the feet of Jesus, wiped His feet with her hair; and the house was filled with the fragrance of the ointment. Judas Iscariot, one of His disciples, who was intending to betray Him, said, "Why was this ointment not sold for three hundred denarii, and given to poor people?" Now he said this, not because he was concerned about the poor, but because he was a thief, and as he had the money box, he used to pilfer what was put into it. Jesus said, "Let her alone, why do you bother her? She has done a good deed to Me. For the poor you will always have with you; and whenever you wish, you can do them good; but you will not always have Me. She has done what she could; she has anointed My body beforehand for the burial. Truly I say to you, wherever the gospel is preached in the whole world, that also which this woman has done shall be spoken of in memory of her."

The great multitude of the Jews learned that He was there; and they came, not for Jesus' sake only, but that they might also see Lazarus, whom He raised from the dead. But the chief priests took counsel that they might put Lazarus to death also; because on account of him many of the Jews were going away, and were believing in Jesus.

Now the feast of the Passover and Unleavened Bread was days off; and the chief priests and the scribes were seeking how to seize Him by stealth, and kill Him; for they were saying, "Not during the festival, lest there be a riot of the people."

Chapter Forty Six

Palm Sunday

After these things, He was going on ahead, ascending to Jerusalem. It came about that when He approached Behphage and Bethany, near the mount that is called Olivet, He sent two of the disciples, saying, "Go into the village opposite you, in which as you enter you will find a colt tied, on which no one yet has ever sat; untie it, and bring it here. And if anyone asks you, 'Why are you untying it?' thus shall you speak, 'The Lord has need of it.' Immediately he will send it back here." Those who were sent went away found it just as He had told them. As they were untying the colt, its owners said to them, "Why are you untying the colt?" And they said, "The Lord has need of it." They gave them permission. They brought it to Jesus, threw their garments on the colt, and put Jesus on it. For it is written, Fear not, daughter of Zion ; behold, your King comes sitting on a donkey's colt. The beast of burden. As He was going, they were spreading their garments in the road. As He was now approaching, near the descent of the Mount of Olives, the whole multitude of the disciples began to praise God joyfully with a loud voice for all the miracles which they had seen. They took the branches of the palm trees, and went out to meet Him, and began to cry out saying, "Hosanna! Blessed is the King who comes in the name of the Lord, even the King of Israel. Blessed is the coming kingdom of our father David. Hosanna in the highest!" Some of the Pharisees in the multitude said to Him, "Teacher, rebuke Your disciples." He answered and said, "I tell you, if these become silent, the stones will cry out!" When He approached, He saw the city and wept over it, saying, "If you had known in this day, even you, the things which make for peace! But now they have been hidden from your eyes. For the days shall come upon you when your enemies will throw up a bank before you, surround you, and hem you in on every side, and will level you to the ground and your children within you, they will not leave you one stone upon another, because you did not recognize the time of your visitation." When He had entered Jerusalem, all the city was stirred, saying, "Who is this?" the multitudes were saying, "This is the prophet Jesus, from Nazareth in Galilee." These things His disciples did not understand at the first; but when Jesus was glorified, then they remembered that these things were written of Him, and that they had done these things to Him.

CHAPTER FORTY SEVEN

MONDAY

He entered Jerusalem and came into the temple; and after looking all around He departed for Bethany with the twelve, since it was already late. On the next day, when they had departed from Bethany, He became hungry. Seeing at a distance a fig tree in leaf, He went to see if perhaps He would find anything on it; and when He came to it, He found nothing but leaves, for it was not the season for figs. He said to it, "May no one ever eat fruit from you again." At once the fig tree withered. And seeing this, the disciples marveled, saying, "How did the fig tree wither at once?" Jesus answered and said to them, "Truly I say to you, if you have faith, and do not doubt, you shall not only do what was done to the fig tree, but even if you say to this mountain, 'Be taken up and cast into the sea,' it shall happen. And everything you ask in prayer, believing, you shall receive."

They came to Jerusalem. He entered the temple and began to cast out those who were buying and selling in the temple, overturned the tables of the moneychangers and the seats of those who were selling doves; and He would not permit anyone to carry goods through the temple. He began to teach and say to them, "Is it not written, 'My house shall be called a house of prayer for all the nations? But you have made it a robber's den." The blind and the lame came to Him in the temple, and He healed them. When the chief priests and the scribes saw the wonderful things that He had done, and the children who were crying out in the temple and saying, "Hosanna to the Son of

David." They became indignant, and said to Him, "Do You hear what these are saying?" Jesus said to them, "Yes; have you never read, 'Out of the mouth of infants and nursing babes Thou hast prepared praise for Thyself'?" The chief priests and the scribes heard this, and began seeking how to destroy Him; for they were afraid of Him, for all the multitude was astonished at His teaching.

Chapter Forty Eight

Tuesday & Wednesday

They came again to Jerusalem, and as He was walking in the temple, the Chief priests, scribes, and elders came to Him, and began saying to Him, "By what authority are You doing these things, or who gave You this authority to do these things?" Jesus said to them, "I will ask you one question, you answer Me, and then I will tell you by what authority I do these things. Was the baptism of John from heaven, or from men? Answer Me." They began reasoning with one another, saying, "If we say, 'From heaven,' He will say, 'Then why did you not believe him?' But shall we say, 'From men'?" they were afraid of the multitude, for all considered John to have been a prophet indeed. Answering Jesus, they said, "We do not know." Jesus said to them, "Neither will I tell you by what authority I do these things. But what do you think? A man had two sons, he came to the first and said, 'Son, go work today in the vineyard.' And he answered and said, 'I will, sir'; and he did not go. He came to the second and said the same thing. But he answered and said, 'I will not'; yet he afterward regretted it and went. Which of the two did the will of his father?" They said, "The latter." Jesus said to them, "Truly I say to you that the tax gatherers and harlots will get into the kingdom of God before you. For John came to you in the way of righteousness and you did not believe him; but the tax gatherers and harlots did believe him; and you, seeing this, did not even feel remorse afterward so as to believe him."

"Listen to another parable. There was a landowner who planted a vineyard and put a wall around it and dug a wine press in it, built a tower, and rented it out to vine growers, and went on a journey. And when the harvest time approached, he sent his slave to the vine growers to receive his produce. The vine growers took his slaves, beat one, killed another, and stoned the third. He sent another group of slaves larger than the first; and they did the same thing to them. But afterward he sent his son to them, saying, 'They will respect my son.' But when the vine growers saw the son, they said among themselves, 'This is the heir; come, let us kill him, and seize his inheritance.' They took him, cast him out of the vineyard, and killed him. Therefore when the owner of the vineyard comes, what will he do to those vine growers?" They said to Him, "He will bring those wretches to a wretched end, and will rent out the vineyard to the other vine growers, who will pay him the proceeds at the proper seasons." Jesus said to them, "Did you never read in the Scriptures, 'The stone which the builders rejected, this became the chief corner stone; this came about from the Lord, and it is marvelous in our eyes'? Therefore I say to you, the kingdom of God will be taken away from you, and be given to a nation producing the fruit of it. He who falls on the stone will be broken to pieces; but on whomever it falls, it will scatter him like dust." When the chief priests and the Pharisees heard His parable, they understood that He was speaking about them. When they sought to seize Him, they became afraid of the multitudes, because they held Him to be a prophet.

Jesus spoke to them again in parables, saying, "The kingdom of heaven may be compared to a King, who gave a wedding feast for his son. He sent out his slave to call those who had been invited to the wedding feast, and they were unwilling to come. Again he sent out other slaves saying 'Tell those who have been invited, "Behold, I have prepared my dinner; my oxen and my fattened livestock are all butchered and everything is ready; come to the wedding feast."' But they paid no attention and went their way, one to his own farm, another to his business, the rest seized his slave, mistreated them and killed them. The king enraged, sent his armies, and destroyed those murderers, and set their city on fire. Then he said to his slaves, 'The wedding is ready, but those who were invited were not worthy. Go therefore to the main highways, and as many as you find there, invite to the wedding feast.' Those slaves went out into the streets, and gathered together all they found, both evil and good; and the wedding hall was filled with dinner guests. But when the king came in to look over the dinner quests, he saw there a man not dressed in wedding clothes, and he said him, 'Friend, how did you come in here without wedding clothes?' He was speechless. Then the king said to the servants, 'Bind him hand and foot, and cast him into the outer darkness; in the place there shall be weeping and gnashing of teeth.' For many are called, but few are chosen."

Chapter Forty Nine

The Pharisees went and counseled together how they might trap Him in what He said, so as to deliver Him up to the rule and the authority of the governor. They sent their disciples to Him, along with the Herodians, saying, "Teacher, we know that You are truthful and teach the way of God in truth, and defer to no one; for You are not partial to any. Tell us therefore, what do You think? Is it lawful to give a poll tax to Caesar, or not? Shall we pay, or shall we not pay?" But Jesus perceived their malice, and said, "Why are you testing Me, you hypocrites? Show Me the coin used for the poll tax." And they brought Him a denarius. He said to them, "Whose likeness and inscription is this?" They said to Him, "Caesar's." Then He said to them, 'Then render to Caesar the things that are Caesar's; and to God the things that are God's." Hearing this, they marveled, and leaving Him, they went away.

Some Sadducees (who say that there is no resurrection) came to Him, and began questioning Him, saying, "Teacher, Moses wrote for us a law that if a man's brother dies, leaves behind a wife, and leaves no child, his brother should take the wife, and raise up offspring to his brother. There were seven brothers; and the first one took a wife, and died, leaving no offspring. The second one took her, and died, leaving behind no offspring; the third likewise; and so all seven left no offspring. Last of all the woman died too. In the resurrection, when they rise again, which one's wife will she be? For all seven had her as a wife." Jesus said to them, "For this reason you are mistaken, that you do not understand the Scriptures, or the power of God? The sons of this age marry and are given in marriage. But those who rise and are resurrected from the dead neither marry, nor are given in marriage; nor neither can they die any more, for they are like angels, and are sons of God, being sons of the resurrection. But regarding the fact that the dead rise again, have you not read in the book of Moses, in the passage about the burning bush, how God spoke to him, saying, 'I am the God of Abraham, the God of Isaac, and the God of Jacob? He is not the God of the dead, but of the living; you are greatly mistaken, for all live to Him." Some of the scribes answered and said, "Teacher, You have spoken well."

When the Pharisees heard that He had put the Sadducees to silence, they gathered themselves together. One of them, a lawyer, asked Him a question, testing Him, "Teacher, which is the great commandment in the law?" He said to him, "The foremost is, 'Hear, O Israel; The Lord our God is one Lord; and you shall love the Lord your God with all your heart, with all your soul, with all your mind, and with all your strength.' The second is this, 'You shall love your neighbor as yourself.' There is no other commandment greater than these. On these two commandments depend the whole Law and the Prophets." The scribe said to Him, "Right, Teacher, You have truly stated that He is One; there is no one else besides Him; to love Him with all the heart and with all the understanding and with all the strength, and to love one's neighbor as himself, is much more than all burnt offerings and sacrifices." When Jesus saw that he had answered intelligently, He said to him, "You are not far from the kingdom of God." After that, no one would venture to ask Him any more questions.

Now while the Pharisees were gathered together, Jesus asked them a question, saying, "What do you think about the Christ, whose son is He?" They said to Him, "The Son of David." He said to them, "Then how does David in the book of Psalms, call Him 'Lord.' Saying, 'The Lord said to my Lord, sit at My right hand, until I put thine enemies beneath feet?' If David then calls Him 'Lord.' How is He his son?" The great crowd enjoyed listening to Him.

While all the people were listening, He said to the disciples, "Beware of the scribes, who like to walk around in long robes, love respectful greetings in the market places, chief seats in the synagogues, and places of honor at banquets, who devour widow's houses, and for appearance's sake offer long prayers; these will receive greater condemnation." Then Jesus spoke to the multitudes saying, "The scribes and the Pharisees have seated themselves in the chair of Moses; therefore all that they tell you, do and observe, but do not do according to their deeds; for they say things, and do not do them. They tie up heavy loads, and lay them on men's shoulders; but they themselves are unwilling to move them with so much as a finger. But they do all their deeds to be noticed by men; for they broaden their phylacteries (small boxes containing Scripture texts worn for religious purposes), and lengthen the tassels of their garments. They love the place of honor at banquets, the chief seats in the synagogues, respectful greetings in the market places, and being called by men, Rabbi. But do not be called Rabbi; for One is your Teacher, and you are all brothers. Do not call anyone on earth your father; for One is your Father, He who is in heaven. Do not be called leaders; for One is your Leader, that is, Christ. But the greatest among you shall be your servant. And whoever exalts himself shall be humbled; and whoever humbles himself shall be exalted.

Woe to you, scribes and Pharisees, hypocrites, because you shut off the kingdom of heaven from men; for you do not enter in yourselves, nor do you allow those who are entering to go in. Woe to you, scribes and Pharisees, hypocrites, because you devour widow's houses, even while for a pretense you make long prayers; therefore you shall receive greater condemnation. Woe to you, scribes and Pharisees, hypocrites, because you travel about on sea and land to make one proselyte; and when he becomes one, you make him twice as much a son of hell as yourselves. Woe to you, blind guides, who say, 'Whoever swears by the temple, that is nothing; but whoever swears by the gold of the temple, he is obligated.' You fools and blind men; which is more important, the gold, or the temple that sanctified the gold? And, 'Whoever swears by the altar, that is nothing, but whoever swears by the offering upon it, he is obligated.' You blind men, which is more important, the offering or the altar that sanctifies the offering? Therefore he who swears, swears both by the altar and by everything on it. And he who swears the temple, swears both by the temple and by Him who dwells within it.

And he who swears by heaven, swears both by the throne of God and by Him who sits upon it. Woe to you, scribes and Pharisees, hypocrites! For you tithe mint, dill, and cumin, and have neglected the weightier provisions of the law; justice and mercy and faithfulness; but these are the things you should have done without neglecting the others. You blind guides, who strain out a gnat and swallow a camel! Woe to you, scribes and Pharisees, hypocrites! For you clean the outside of the cup and of the dish, but inside they are full of robbery and self-indulgence. You blind Pharisee, first clean the inside of the cup and of the dish, so that the outside of it may become clean also. Woe to you, scribes and Pharisees, and hypocrites! For you are like whitewashed tombs which on the outside appear beautiful, but inside they are full of dead men's bones and all uncleanness. Even so you too outwardly appear righteous to men, but inwardly you are full of hypocrisy and lawlessness. Woe to you, scribes and Pharisees, hypocrites! For you build the tombs of the prophets, adorn the monuments of the righteous, and say, 'If we had been living in the days of our father, we would not have been partners with them in shedding the blood of the prophets.' Consequently you bear witness against yourselves, that you are sons of those who murdered the prophets. Fill up then the measure of the guilt of your fathers. you serpents, you brood of vipers, how shall you escape the sentence of hell? Behold, I am sending you prophets, wise men, and scribes; some of them you will kill and crucify, and some of them you will scourge in your synagogues, and persecute from city to city, that upon you may fall the guilt of all the righteous blood shed on earth, from the blood of righteous Abel to the blood of Zechariah, the son of Berechiah, who you murdered between the temple and the altar. Truly I say to you, all these things shall come upon this generation. O Jerusalem, Jerusalem, who kills the prophets and stones whose who are sent to her! How often I wanted to gather your children together, the way a hen gathers her chicks under her wings, and you were unwilling. Behold, your house is being left to you desolate! For I say to you, from now on you shall not see Me until you say, 'Blessed is He who comes in the name of the Lord!'"

He looked up and saw the rich putting their gifts into the treasury. And He saw a certain poor widow putting in two small copper coins which amounts to a cent. He said, "Truly I say to you, this poor widow put in more than all of them; for they put in the offering all out of their surplus; but she out of her poverty put in all that she had to live on."

CHAPTER FIFTY

N ow there were certain Greeks among those who were going up to worship at the feast; these came to Philip, who was from Bethsaida of Galilee, and began to ask him saying, "Sir, we wish to see Jesus." Philip came and told Andrew; Andrew and Philip came, and they told Jesus. Jesus answered them, saying, "The hour has come for the Son of Man to be glorified. Truly, truly, I say to you, unless a grain of wheat falls into the earth and dies, it remains by itself alone; but it dies, it bears much fruit. He who loves his life loses it; and he who hates his life in this world shall keep it to life eternal. If any one serves Me, let him follow Me; and where I am, there shall My servant also be; if any one serves Me, the Father will honor him. Now My soul has become troubled; and what shall I say, 'Father, save Me from this hour'? But for this purpose I came to this hour." "Father, glorify Thy name." There came a voice out of heaven; "I have both glorified it, and will glorify it again." The multitude, who stood by and heard it, were saying that it had thundered; others were saying, "An angel has spoken to Him." Jesus answered and said, "This voice has not come for My sake, but for your sakes. Now judgment is upon this world; now the ruler of this world shall be cast out. And I, if I be lifted up from the earth, will draw all men to Myself." He was saying this to indicate the kind of death by which He was to die. The multitude answered Him, "We have heard out of the Law that the Christ is to remain forever; and how can You say, 'The Son of Man must be lifted up?' Who is this Son of Man?" Jesus said to them, "For a little while longer the light is among you. Walk while you have the light, that darkness may not overtake you; he who walks in the darkness does not know where he goes. While you have the light, believe in the light, in order that you may become sons of light."

Thou He had performed so many signs before them, yet they were not believing in Him; that the word of Isaiah the prophet might be fulfilled, which he spoke, "Lord, who has believed our report? And to whom has the arm of the Lord been revealed?" For this cause they could not believe, for Isaiah said again, "He has blinded their eyes, and He hardened their heart; lest they see with their eyes, and perceive with their heart, and be converted, and I heal them." These things Isaiah said, because he saw His glory, and he spoke of Him. Nevertheless many of the rulers believed in Him, but because of the Pharisees they were not confessing Him, lest they should be put out of the synagogue; for they loved the approval of men rather than the approval of God. Jesus cried out and said, "He who believes in Me does not believe in Me, but in Him who sent Me. And he who beholds Me beholds the One who sent Me. I have come as light into the world, that everyone who believes in Me may not remain in darkness. And if any one hears My saying, and does not keep them, I do not judge him; for I did not come to judge the world, but to save the world. He who rejects Me, and does not receive My sayings, has one who judges him; the word I spoke is what will judge him at the last day. For I did not speak on My own initiative, but the Father Himself who sent Me has given Me commandment, what to say, and what to speak. I know that His commandment is eternal life; therefore the things I speak, I speak just as the Father has told Me."

Now during the day He was teaching in the temple, but at evening He would go out and spend the night on the mount that is called Olivet. While some were talking about the temple, that it was adorned with beautiful stones and votive gifts, He said, "As for these things which you are looking at, the days will come in which there will not be left one stone upon another which will not be torn down." As He was sitting on the Mount of Olives opposite the temple, Peter, James, John, and Andrew were questioning Him, saying, "Teacher, when will these things be? And what will be the sign when these things are about to take place?" He said, "Take heed that you be not misled; For many will come in My name, saying, 'I am He,' and, 'The time is at hand': do not go after them, they will mislead many. When you hear of wars and disturbances, do not be terrified; for these things must take place first, but the end does not follow immediately." Then He continued by saying to them, "Nation will rise against nation, kingdom against kingdom, there will be great earthquakes, in various places plagues and famines; and there will be terrors and great signs from heaven. These things are merely the beginning of birth pangs. But before all these things, they will lay their hands on you and will persecute you, delivering you to the synagogues and persons, bringing you before kings and governors for My name's sake. It will lead to an opportunity for your testimony. **The gospel** must first be preached to all the nations. So make up your minds not to prepare beforehand to defend yourselves; for I will give you utterance and wisdom which none of your opponents will be able to resist or refute. But you will be betrayed even by parents, brothers, relatives, and friends, and they will put some of you to death, and you will be hated by all on account of My name. And because lawlessness is increased, most people's love will grow cold. Yet not a hair of your head will perish. By your perseverance you will win your souls. **This gospel** of the kingdom shall be preached in the whole world for a witness to all the nations, and then the end shall come."

"When you see Jerusalem surrounded by armies, then recognize that her desolation is at hand. When you see the abomination of desolation which was spoken of through Daniel the prophet, standing in the holy place (let the reader understand), then let those who are in Judea flee to the mountains, let him who is on the housetop not go down to get the things out that are in his house; and let him who is in the field not turn back to get his cloak. These are days of vengeance, in order that all things which are written may be fulfilled. But woe to those who are with child and to those who nurse babes in those days! There will be great distress upon the land, and wrath to this people, they will fall by the edge of the sword, and will be led captive into all the nations; and Jerusalem will be trampled underfoot by the Gentiles until the times of the Gentiles be fulfilled. But pray that your flight may not be in the winter, or on a Sabbath; for then there will be a great tribulation, such as has not occurred since the beginning of the world until now, nor ever shall. And unless those days had been cut short, no life would have been saved; but for the sake of the elect those days shall be cut short. If any one says to you, 'Behold, here is the Christ,' or 'There He is,' do not believe him. For false Christs and false prophets will arise and will show great signs and wonders, so as to mislead, if possible, even the elect. Behold, I have told you in advance. If they say to you, 'Behold, He is in the wilderness,' do not go forth, or, 'Behold, He is in the inner rooms,' do not believe them. For just as the lightning comes from the east, and flashes even to the west, so shall the coming of the Son of Man be. Wherever the corpse is, there the vultures will gather. But immediately after the tribulation of those days the sun will be darkened, and the moon will not give its light, the stars will fall from the sky, and upon the earth dismay among nations, in perplexity at the roaring of the sea and the waves. Men will faint from fear and the expectation of the things which are coming upon the world, the powers of the heavens will be shaken, then the sign of the Son of Man will appear in the sky, then will the tribes of the earth will mourn, and they will see the Son of Man coming on the clouds of the sky with power and great glory. He will send forth His angels with a great trumpet and they will gather together His elect from the four winds, from one end of the sky to the other. But when these things begin to take place, straighten up and lift up your heads, because your redemption is drawing near.

Now learn the parable from the fig tree; when its branch as already become tender, and puts forth its leaves, you know the summer is near; even so you too, when you see all these things recognize that He is near, right at the door. Truly I say to you, this generation will not pass away until all these things take place. Heaven and earth will pass away, but My words shall not pass away. But of that day and hour no one knows, not even the angels of heaven, nor the Son, but the Father alone. For the coming of the Son of Man will be just like the days of Noah. For as in those days which were before the flood they were eating and drinking, they were marrying and giving in marriage, until the day that Noah entered the ark, and they did not understand until the flood came and took them all away, so shall the coming of the Son of Man be. Take heed, be on the alert, for you do not know when the appointed time of your Lords coming. It is like a man, away on a journey, who upon leaving his house and putting his slaves in charge, assigning to each one his task, also commanded the doorkeeper to stay on the alert. Therefore, be on the alert, for you do not know when the master of the house is coming, whether in the evening, at midnight, at cockcrowing, or in the morning, lest he come suddenly and find you asleep. Be on guard, that your hearts may not be weighted down with dissipation, drunkenness, and the worries of life, and that day come on you suddenly like a trap; for it will come upon all those who dwell on the face of all the earth. But keep on the alert at all times, praying in order that you may have strength to escape all these things that are about to take place, and to stand before the Son of Man. And what I say to you I say to all, 'Be on the alert'" He told a parable saying, "The kingdom of heaven will be comparable to ten virgins who took their lamps, and went out to meet the bridegroom. Five of them were foolish, and five were prudent. For when the foolish took their lamps, they took no oil with them, but the prudent took oil in flasks along with their lamps. Now while the bridegroom was delaying, they all got drowsy and began to sleep. But at midnight there was a shout, 'Behold, the bridegroom! Come out to meet him.' Then all those virgins arose, and trimmed their lamps. The foolish said to the prudent, 'Give us some of your oil, for our lamps are going out.' But the prudent answered, saying, 'No, there will not be enough for us and you too; go instead to the dealers and buy some for yourselves.' While they were going away to make the purchase, the bridegroom came, those who were ready went in with him to the wedding feast; and the door was shut. And later the other virgins also came, saying, 'Lord, Lord, open up for us.' But he answered and said, 'Truly I say to you, I do not know you.' Be on the alert then for you do not know the day nor the hour."

CHAPTER FIFTY ONE

He continued teaching them, saying, "When the Son of Man comes in His glory, and all the angels with Him, then He will sit on His glorious throne. All the nations will be gathered before Him; He will separate them from one another, as the shepherd separates the sheep from the goats; He will put the sheep on His right, and goats on the left. Then the King will say to those on His right, 'Come, you who are blessed of My Father, inherit the kingdom prepared for you from the foundation of the world. For I was hungry, and you gave Me something to eat; I was thirsty, and you gave Me drink; I was a stranger, and you invited Me in; naked, and you clothed Me; I was sick, and you visited Me; I was in prison, and you came to Me.' Then the righteous will answer Him, saying, 'Lord, when did we see You hungry, and feed You, or thirsty, and give You drink? When did we see You a stranger, and invite You in, or naked, and clothed You? When did we see You sick, or in prison, and come to You?' The King will answer and say to them, 'Truly I say to you, to the extent that you did it to one of these brothers of Mine, even the least of them, you did it to Me.' Then He will also say to those on His left, 'Depart from Me, accursed ones, into the eternal fire which has been prepared for the devil and his angels; for I was hungry, and you gave Me nothing to eat; I was thirsty, and you gave Me nothing to drink; I was a stranger, and you did not invite Me in; naked, and you did not clothe Me; sick, and in prison, and you did not visit Me.' Then they themselves also will answer, saying, 'Lord, when did we see You hungry, or thirst, or a stranger, or naked, or sick, or in prison, and did not take care or You?'

Then He will answer them, saying, 'Truly I say to you, to the extent that you did not do it to one of the least of these, you did not do it to Me.' And these will go away into eternal punishment, but the righteous into eternal life."

CHAPTER FIFTY TWO

It came about that when Jesus had finished all these words, He said to His disciples, "You know that after two days the Passover is coming, and the Son of Man is to be delivered up for crucifixion." Then the chief priests and the elders of the people were gathered together in the court of the high priest, named Caiaphas; they plotted together to seize Jesus by stealth, and kill Him. Now Satan entered into one of the twelve, named Judas Iscariot, who went to the chief priests, and said, "What are you willing to give me to deliver Him up to you?" They weighed out to him thirty pieces of silver. From then on he began looking for a good opportunity to betray Him.

THURSDAY

Then came the day of Unleavened Bread on which the Passover lamb had to be sacrificed. He sent Peter and John, saying, "Go and prepare the Passover for us, that we may eat it." And they said to Him, "Where do You want us to prepare it?" He said to them, "Behold, when you have entered the city, a man will meet you carrying a pitcher of water; follow him into the house that he enters. And you shall say to the owner of the house, 'The Teacher says to you, "Where is the guest room in which I may eat the Passover with My disciples?" ' He will show you a large, furnished, upper room; prepare it there." They departed and found everything just as He had told them; and they prepared the Passover. When the hour had come He came with the rest of the twelve and reclined at table. He said to them, "I have earnestly desired to eat this Passover with you before I suffer; for I say to you, I shall never again eat it until it is fulfilled in the kingdom of God." Having taken a cup, when He had given thanks, He said, "Take this and share it among yourselves; for I say to you, I will not drink of the fruit of the vine from now on until the kingdom of God comes." And having taken some bread, when He had given thanks, He broke it, and gave it to them, saying, "This is My body which is given for you; do this in remembrance of Me." In the same way He took the cup after they had eaten, saying, "This cup which is poured out for you is the new covenant in My blood." After singing a hymn, Jesus said to them, "You will all fall away, because it is written, 'I will strike down the shepherd, and the sheep shall be scattered.' But after I have been raised, I will go before you to Galilee."

There arose also a dispute among them as to which one of them was revered to be greatest. He said to them, "The kings of the Gentiles lord it over them; and those who have authority over them are called 'Benefactors.' But not so with you, but let him who is the greatest among you become as the youngest, and the leader as the servant. For who is greater, the one who reclines at table, or the one who serves? Is it not the one who reclines at table? But I am among you as the one who serves. You are those who have stood by Me in My trials; and just as My Father has granted Me a kingdom, I grant you that you may eat and drink at My table in My kingdom, and you will sit on thrones judging the twelve tribes of Israel."

"Now before the Feast of the Passover, Jesus knowing that His hour had come that He should depart out this world to the Father, having loved His own who were in the world, He loved them to the end. During supper, the devil having already put into the heart of Judas Iscariot, the son of Simon, to betray Him, Jesus, knowing that the Father had given all things into His hands, that He had come forth from God, and was going back to God, rose from supper, and laid aside His garments; and taking a towel with which He was girded. So He came to Simon Peter. He said to Him, "Lord, do You wash my feet?" Jesus answered and said to him, "What I do you do not realize now;

but you shall understand hereafter." Peter said to Him, "Never shall You wash my feet!" Jesus answered him, "If I do not wash you, you have no part with Me." Simon Peter said to Him, "Lord, not my feet only, but also my hands and my head." Jesus said to him, "He who has bathed needs only to wash his feet, but is completely clean; and you are clean, but not all of you." For He knew the one who was betraying Him; for this reason He said, "Not all of you are clean." And so when He had washed their feet, taken His garments, and reclined at table again, He said to them, "Do you know what I have done for you? You call Me Teacher and Lord; and you are right; for so I am. If I then, the Lord and the Teacher, washed your feet, you also ought to wash one another's feet. For I gave you an example that you also should do as I did to you. Truly, truly, I say to you, a slave is not greater that his master; neither one who is sent greater than the one who sent him. If you know these things, you are blessed if you do them."

"I do not speak of all of you. I know the ones I have chosen; but it is that the Scripture may be fulfilled, 'He who eats My bread has lifted up his heel against Me.' From now on I am telling you before it comes to pass, so that when it does occur, you may believe that I am He. Truly, truly, I say to you, he who receives whomever I send receives Me; and he who receives Me receives Him who sent Me." When Jesus had said this, He became troubled in spirit, testified, and said, "Truly, truly, I say to you, that one of you will betray Me. Behold, the hand of the one betraying Me is with Me on the table. For indeed, the Son of Man is going as it has been determined; but woe to that man through whom He is betrayed! It would have been good for that man if he had not been born." The disciples began looking at one another, at a loss to know of which one He was speaking. There was reclining on Jesus' breast one of His disciples, whom Jesus loved. Simon Peter gestured to him, and said to him, "Tell us who it is of whom He is speaking." He leaning back thus on Jesus' breast, said to Him, "Lord, who is it?" Jesus answered, "That is the one for whom I shall dip the morsel and give it to him." So when He had dipped the morsel, He took and gave it to Judas, the son of Simon Iscariot. And after the morsel, Satan then entered into him. Jesus said to him, "What you do, do quickly." Now no one of those reclining at table knew for what purpose He had said this to him. For some were supposing, because Judas had the money box, that Jesus was saying to him, "But the things we have need of for the feast"; or else, that he should give something to the poor. So after receiving the morsel he went out immediately; and it was night. When he had gone out, Jesus said, "Now is the Son of Man glorified, and God is glorified in Him; if God is glorified in Him, God will also glorify Him in Himself, and will glorify Him immediately. Little children, I am with you a little while longer. You shall seek Me; and as I said to the Jews, 'Where I am going, you cannot come,' now I say to you also. A new commandment I give to you, that you love one another, even as I have loved you, that you also love one another. By this all men will know that you are My disciples, if you have love for one another." Simon Peter said to Him, "Lord, where are You going?" Jesus answered, "Where I go, you cannot follow Me now; but you shall follow later." Peter said to Him, "Lord, why can I not follow You right now? I will lay down my life for You." Jesus answered, "Will you lay down your life for Me? Simon, Simon, behold, Satan has demanded permission to sift you like wheat; but I have prayed for you, that your faith may not fail; and you, when once you have turned again, strengthen your brothers. I tell you, Peter, the cock will not crow today until you have denied three times that you know Me."

He said to them, "When I sent you out without purse, bag and sandals, you did not lack anything, did you?" They said, "No, nothing," He said to them, "But now let him who has a purse take it along, likewise also a bag, and let him who has no sword sell his robe and buy one. For I tell you, that this which is written must be fulfilled in Me, 'And He was classed among criminals'; for this which refers to Me has its fulfillment."

CHAPTER FIFTY THREE

Jesus told his disciples, "Let not your heart be troubled; believe in God, believe also in Me. In My Father's house are many dwelling places; if it were not so, I would have told you; for I go to prepare a place for you. If I go and prepare a place for you, I will come again, and receive you to Myself; that where I am, there you may be also. And you know the way where I am going." Thomas said to Him, "Lord, we do not know where You are going; how do we know the way?" Jesus said to him, "I am the way, the truth, and the life; no one comes to the Father, but through Me. If you had known Me, you would have known My Father also; from now on you know Him, and have seen Him." Philip said to Him, "Lord, show us the Father, and it is enough for us." Jesus said to him, "Have I been so long with you, and yet you have not come to know Me, Philip? He who had seen Me has seen the Father; how do you say, 'Show us the Father'? Do you not believe that I am in the Father, and the Father is in Me? The words that I say to you I do not speak on My own initiative, but the Father abiding in Me does His works. Believe Me that I am in the Father, and the Father in Me; otherwise believe on account of the works themselves. Truly, truly, I say to you, he who believes in Me, the works that I do shall he do also; and greater works than these shall he do; because I go to the Father."

"Whatever you ask in My name, that will I do, that the Father may be glorified in the Son. If you ask Me anything in My name, I will do it. If you love Me, you will keep My commandments. I will ask the Father, and He will give you another Helper, that He may be with you forever; that is the Spirit of truth, whom the world cannot receive, because it does not behold Him or know Him, but you know Him because He abides with you, and will be in you. I will not leave you as orphans; I will come to you. After a little while the world will behold Me no more; but you will behold Me; because I live, you shall live also. In that day you shall know that I am in My father, and you in Me, and I in you. He who has My commandments and keeps them, he who loves Me shall be loved by My Father, and I will love him, and will disclose Myself to him." Judas (not Iscariot) said to Him, "Lord, what then has happened that You are going to disclose Yourself to us, and not to the world?" Jesus answered and said to him, "If anyone Loves Me, he will keep My word; and My Father will love him, and We will come to him, and make Our abode with him. He who does not love Me does not keep My words; the word which you hear is not Mine, but the Father's who sent Me. These things I have spoken to you, while abiding with you. But the Helper, the Holy Spirit, whom the Father will send in My name, He will teach you all things, and bring to your remembrance all that I said to you. Peace I leave with you; My peace I give to you; not as the world gives, do I give to you. Let not your heart be troubled, nor let it be fearful. You heard that I said to you, 'I go away, and I will come to you.' If you loved Me, you would have rejoiced because I go to the Father; for the Father is greater than I. Now I have told you before it comes to pass, that when it comes to pass, you may believe. I will not speak much more with you, for the ruler of the world is coming, and he has nothing in Me; but that the world may know that I love the Father, and as the Father gave Me commandment, even so I do."

"I am the true vine, and My Father is the vinedresser. Every branch in Me that does not bear fruit, He takes away; and every branch that bears fruit, He prunes it, that it may bear more fruit. You are already clean because of the word which I have spoken to you. Abide in Me, and I in you. As the branch cannot bear fruit of itself, unless it abides in the vine, so neither can you, unless you abide in Me. I am the vine, you are the branches; he who abides in Me, and I in him, he bears much fruit; for apart from Me you can do nothing. If anyone does not abide in Me, he is thrown away as a branch, dries up; they gather them, cast them into the fire, and they are burned. If you abide in Me, and My words abide in you, ask whatever you wish, and it shall be done for you. By this is My Father glorified, that you bear much fruit, and so prove to be My disciples. Just as the Father has loved Me, I have also loved you; abide in My love. If you keep My commandments, you will abide in My love; just as I have kept My Father's commandments, and abide in His love. These things I have spoken to you, that My joy may be in you, and that your joy may be made full. This is My commandment, that you love one another, just as I have loved you. Greater love has no one than this, that one lay down his life for his friends. You are My friends, if you do what I command you. No longer do I call you slaves; for the slave does not know what his master is doing; but I have called you friends, for all things that I have heard from My Father I have made known to you. You did not choose Me, but I chose you, and appointed you, that you should go and bear fruit, and that your fruit should remain, that whatever you ask of the Father in My name, He may give to you. This I command you, that you love one another. If the world hates you, you know that it has hated Me before it hated you. If you were of the world, the world would love its own; but because you are not of the world, but I chose you out of the world, therefore the world hates you. Remember the word that I said to you, 'A slave is not greater than his master.'"

"If they persecuted Me, they will also persecute you; if they kept My word, they will keep yours also. But all these things they will do to you for My name's sake, because they do not know the One who sent Me. If I had not come and spoken to them, they would not have sin, but now they have no excuse for their sin. He who hates Me hates My Father also. If I had not done among them, the works which no one else did, they would not have sin; but now they have both seen and hated Me and My Father as well. But they have done this in order that the word may be fulfilled that is written in their Law, 'They hated Me without a cause.'"

"When the Helper comes, whom I will send to you from the Father, that is the Spirit of truth, who proceeds from the Father, He will bear witness of Me, and you will bear witness also, because you have been with Me from the beginning. These things I have spoken to you, that you may be kept from stumbling. They will make you outcasts from the synagogue; but an hour is coming for everyone who kills you, to think that he is offering service to God. These things they will do, because they have not known the Father, or Me. But these things I have spoken to you, that when their hour comes, you may remember that I told you of them. These things I did not say to you at the beginning, because I was with you. But now I am going to Him who sent Me; and none of you asks Me, 'Where are You going?' But because I have said these things to you, sorrow has filled your heart. But I tell you the truth, it is to your advantage that I go away; for if I do not go away, the Helper shall not come to you; but if I go, I will send Him to you. And He, when He comes, will convict the world concerning sin, righteousness, and judgment; because they do not believe in Me; and because the ruler of this world has been judged. I have many more things to say to you, but you cannot bear them now. But when He, the Spirit of truth, comes, He will guide you into all the truth; for He will not speak on His own initiative; but whatever He hears, He will speak; and He will disclose to you what is to come. He shall glorify Me; for He shall take of Mine, and shall disclose it to you."

"All things that the Father has are Mine; therefore I said, that He takes of Mine, and will disclose it to you. A little while, and you will no longer behold Me; and again a little while, and you will see Me." Some of His disciples said to one another, "What is these things He is telling us, 'A little while, and you will not behold Me; and again a little while, and you will see Me'; and 'Because I go to the Father'?" So they were saying, "What is this that He says, 'A little while'? We do not know what He is talking about." Jesus knew that they wished to question Him, and He said to them, "Are you deliberating together about this, that I said, 'A little while, and you will not behold Me, and again a little while, and you will see Me'? Truly, truly, I say to you, that you will weep and lament, but the world will rejoice; you will be sorrowful, but your sorrow will be turned to joy. Whenever a woman is in travail she has sorrow, because her hour has come; but when she gives birth to the child, she remembers the anguish no more, for joy that a child has been born into the world. You, too, now have sorrow; but I will see you again, your heart will rejoice, and no one takes your joy away from you. In that day you will ask Me no question."

"Truly, truly, I say to you, if you shall ask the Father for anything, He will give it to you in My name. Until now you have asked for nothing in My name; ask, and you will receive, that your joy may be made full. These things I have spoken to you in figurative language; an hour is coming, when I will speak no more to you in figurative language, but will tell you plainly of the Father. In that day you will ask in My name; and I do not say to you that I will request the Father on your behalf; for the Father Himself loves you, because you have loved Me, and have believed that I came forth from the Father. I came forth from the Father, and have come into the world; I am leaving the world again, and going to the Father." His disciples said, "Lo, now You are speaking plainly, and are not using a figure of speech. Now we know that You know all things, and have no need for anyone to question You; by this we believe that You came from God." Jesus answered them, "Do you now believe? Behold, an hour is coming, and has already come, for you to be scattered, each to his own home, and to leave Me alone; and yet I am not alone, because the Father is with Me. These things I have spoken to you, that in Me you may have peace. In the world you have tribulation, But take courage; I have overcome the world."

Chapter Fifty Four

These things Jesus spoke; and lifting up His eyes to heaven, He said, "Father, the hour has come; glorify Thy Son, that the Son may glorify Thee, even as Thou gavest Him authority over all mankind, that to all whom Thou hast given Him, He may give eternal life. This is eternal life, that they may know Thee, the only true God, and Jesus Christ Whom Thou hast sent. I glorified Thee on the earth, having accomplished the work which Thou hast given Me to do. Now, glorify Thou Me together with Thyself, Father, with the glory which I ever had with Thee before the world was. I manifested Thy name to the men whom Thou gavest Me out of the world; Thine they were, and Thou gavest them to Me, and they have kept Thy word. Now they have come to know that everything Thou hast given Me is from Thee; for the words which Thou gavest Me I have given to them; they received them, and truly understood that I came forth from Thee, and they believed that Thou didst send Me. I ask on their behalf; I do not ask on behalf of the world, but of those whom Thou hast given Me; for they are Thine; and all things that are Mine are Thine, and Thine are Mine; and I have been glorified in them. I am no more in the world; yet they themselves are in the world; and I come to Thee. Holy Father, keep them in Thy name, the name which Thou hast given Me, that they may be one, even as We are. While I was with them, I was keeping them in Thy name which Thou hast given Me; I guarded them, and not one of them perished but the son of perdition, that the Scripture might be fulfilled. But now I come to Thee; and these things I speak in the world, that they may have My joy made full in themselves. I have given them Thy word; and the world has hated them, because they are not of the world, even as I am not of the world. I do not ask Thee to take them out of the world, but to keep them from the evil one. They are not of the world, even as I am not of the world. Sanctify them in the truth; Thy word is truth. As Thou didst send Me into the world, I also have sent them into the world. For their sakes I sanctify Myself, that they themselves also may be sanctified I truth. I do not ask in behalf of these alone, but for those also who believe in Me through their word; that they may all be one; even as Thou, Father, are in Me, and I in Thee, that they also may be in Us; that the world may believe that Thou didst send Me. The glory which Thou hast given Me I have given to them; that they may be one, just as We are one; I in Thee, and Thou in Me, that they may be perfected in unity, that the world may know that Thou didst send Me, and didst love them, even as Thou didst love Me. Father, I desire that they also, whom Thou hast given Me, be with Me where I am, in order that they may behold My glory, which Thou hast given Me; for Thou didst love Me before the foundation of the world. O righteous Father, although the world has not known Thee, yet I have known Thee; and these have known that Thou didst send Me; and I have made Thy name known to them, and will make it known; that the love wherewith Thou didst love Me may be in them, and I in them."

CHAPTER FIFTY FIVE

When Jesus had spoken these words, He went forth with His disciples over the ravine of the Kidron, where there was a garden, they came to a place named Gethsemane; and He said to His disciples, "Sit here until I have prayed." He took with Him Peter and James and John and began to be very distressed and troubled. He said to them, "My soul is deeply grieved to the point of death; remain here and keep watch." He went a little beyond them, fell to the ground, and began praying that if it were possible, the hour might pass Him by. He was saying, "Abba! Father! All things are possible for Thee; remove this cup from Me; yet not what I will, but what Thou wilt." Now an angel from heaven appeared to Him, strengthening Him. Being in agony He was praying very fervently; and His sweat became like drops of blood, falling down upon the ground. He returned to His disciples, and found them sleeping, and said to Peter, "Simon, are you asleep? Could you not keep watch for one hour? Keep watching and praying, that you may not come into temptation; the spirit is willing, but the flesh is weak" Again He went away and prayed, saying, "My Father, if this cannot pass away unless I drink it, Thy will be done." Again He came and found them sleeping, for their eyes were every heavy; and they did not know what to answer Him. He came the third time, and said to them, "Are you still sleeping and taking your rest? It is enough; the hour has come; behold, the Son of Man is being betrayed into the hands of sinners. Arise, let us be going; behold, the one who betrays Me is at hand!"

Now Judas who was betraying Him knew the place; for Jesus had often met there with His disciples. Judas then, having received the

Roman cohort, officers from the chief priests, and the Pharisees, came there with lanterns, torches and weapons. Jesus, knowing all the things that were coming upon Him, went forth, and said to them, "Whom do you seek?" They answered Him, "Jesus the Nazarene." He said to them, "I am He." Judas who was betraying Him, was standing with them. When He said to them, "I am He." They drew back, and fell to the ground. Again He asked them, "Whom do you seek?" And they said, "Jesus the Nazarene." Jesus answered, "I told you that I am He; if therefore you seek Me, let these go their way," that the word might be fulfilled which He spoke, "Of those whom Thou hast given Me I lost not one." Now he who was betraying Him had given them a signal, saying, "Whomever I shall kiss, He is the one; seize Him, and lead Him away under guard." While Jesus was still speaking, Judas went up to Him, saying, "Rabbi!" and kissed Him. Jesus said to him, "Judas, are you betraying the Son of Man with a kiss? Friend, do what you have come for." They laid hands on Him, and seized Him. Now behold, Simon Peter, one of those who were with Jesus reached and drew out his sword, struck the slave of the high priest, and cut off his right ear, the slaves name was Malchus. Jesus said to him, "Put your sword back into its place; for all those who take up the sword shall perish by the sword. Or do you think that I cannot appeal to My Father, and He will at once put at My disposal more than twelve legions of angels? How then shall the Scriptures be fulfilled, that it must happen this way?" He touched the slave's ear and it was healed. At that time Jesus said to the multitudes, "Have you come out with swords and clubs to arrest Me as though I were a robber? Every day I used to sit in the temple teaching and you did not seize Me. But all this has taken place that the Scriptures of the prophets may be fulfilled." A certain young man was following Him, wearing nothing but a linen sheet over his naked body; and they seized him. But he left the linen sheet behind, and escaped naked. They led Jesus away to Caiaphas, the high priest; all the chief priests, the elders and scribes gathered together.

Chapter Fifty Six

Good Friday

The Roman cohort and the commander, and the officers of the Jews, arrested Jesus, bound Him, and led Him, to Anna first; for he was father-in-law of Caiaphas, who was high priest that year. Now Caiaphas was the one who had advised the Jews that it was expedient for one man to die on behalf of the people. Peter had followed Him at a distance, and so was another disciple. Now that disciple was known to the high priest, and entered with Jesus into the court of the high priest but Peter was standing at the door outside. So the other disciple, who was known to the high priest, went out and spoke to the doorkeeper, brought in Peter, and he was sitting with the officers, and warming himself at the fire. Now the chief priests and the whole Council kept trying to obtain testimony against Jesus to put Him to death; and they were finding none. For many were giving false testimony against Him, and yet their testimony was not consistent. Some stood up and began to give false testimony against Him, saying, "We heard Him say, 'I will destroy this temple made with hands, and in three days I will build another made without hands.'" And not even in this respect was their testimony consistent. The high priest arose and came forward and questioned Jesus, saying, "Do You make no answer to what these men are testifying against You?" But He kept silent, and made no answer. Again the high priest was questioning Him, about His disciples, and about His teaching. Jesus answered him, "I have spoken openly to the world; I always taught in synagogues, and in the temple, where all the

Jews come together; and I spoke nothing in secret. Why do you question Me? Question those who have heard what I spoke to them; behold, these know what I said." The high priest said to Him, "I adjure You by the living God, that You tell us whether You are the Christ, the Son of the Blessed One?" Jesus said, "You have said it yourself; nevertheless I tell You, I am; and you shall see the Son of Man sitting at the right hand of power, and coming with the clouds of heaven." Tearing his clothes, the high priest said, "What further need do we have of witnesses? You have heard the blasphemy; how does it seem to you?" They all condemned Him to be deserving of death. Some began to spit at Him, to blindfold Him, and beat Him, with their fist, to say to Him, "Prophesy to us, You Christ; who is the one who is hitting you?" The officers received Him with slaps in the face. Anna sent Him bound to Caiaphas the high priest.

Now the slaves and the officers were standing there, having made a charcoal fire, for it was cold and they were warming themselves. Peter was below in the courtyard, one of the servant girls of the high priest came, being a relative of the one whose ear Peter cut off, and seeing Peter warming himself, she looked at him, and said, 'Did I not see you in the garden with Him? You, too, were with Jesus the Nazarene." But He denied it, saying, 'I neither know nor understand what you are talking about." He went out onto the porch. The maid saw him, and began once more to say to the bystanders, "This is one of them!" Again he was denying it. After a little while the bystanders were again saying to Peter, "Surely you are one of them, for you are a Galilean too." But he began to curse and swear, "I do not know this fellow you are talking about!" And immediately a cock crowed a second time. The Lord turned and looked at Peter. Peter remembered how Jesus had made the remark to him, "Before the a cock crows twice, you will deny Me three times." He went outside and began to weep bitterly.

They led Jesus from Caiaphas into the Praetorium; it was early; and they themselves did not enter into the Praetorium in order that they might not be defiled, but might eat the Passover. Pilate the governor therefore went out to them, and said, "What accusation do you bring against this Man?" They answered and said to him, "If this Man were not an evildoer, we would not have delivered Him up to you. We found this man misleading our nation and forbidding to pay taxes to Caesar, and saying He Himself is Christ, a King." Pilate said to them, "Take Him yourselves, and judge Him according to your law." The Jews said to him, "We are not permitted to put any one to death," that the word of Jesus might be fulfilled, which He spoke, signifying by what kind of death He was about to die. Pilate entered again into the Praetorium, summoned Jesus, and said to Him, "You are the King of the Jews?" Jesus answered, "Are you saying this on your own initiative, or did others tell you about Me?" Pilate answered, "I am not a Jew, am I? Your own nation and the chief priests delivered You up to me; what have You done?" Jesus answered, "My kingdom is not of this world. If My kingdom were of this world, then My servants would be fighting, that I might not be delivered up to the Jews; but as it is, My kingdom is not of this realm." Pilate said to Him, "So you are a king?" Jesus answered, "It is as you say. You say correctly that I am a king. For this I have been born, and for this I have come into the world, to bear witness to the truth. Every one who is of the truth hears My voice." Pilate said to Him, "What is truth?" Pilate asked whether the man was a Galilean. When he learned that He belonged to Herod's jurisdiction, he sent Him to Herod, who himself also was in Jerusalem at that time.

Now Herod was very glad when he saw Jesus; for he had wanted to see Him for a long time, because he had been hearing about Him and was hoping to see some sign performed by Him. He questioned Him at some length; but He answered him nothing. The chief priests and the scribes were standing there, accusing Him vehemently. Herod with his soldiers, after treating Him with contempt and mocking Him, sent Him, back to Pilate. Now Herod and Pilate became friends with one another that very day; for before they had been at enmity with each other.

Pilate summoned the chief priests, the ruler and the people, and said to them, "You brought this man to me as one who incites the people to rebellion, and behold, having examined Him before you, I have found no guilt in this man regarding the charges which you make against Him. No, nor has Herod, for he sent Him back to us; and behold, nothing deserving death had been done by Him. I will therefore punish Him and release Him." But they kept on insisting, saying, "He stirs up the people, teaching all over Judea, starting from Galilee, even as far as this place." Pilate said to them, "You have a custom, that I should release someone for you at the Passover; do you wish then that I release for you King of the Jews?" They cried out again, saying, "Not this Man, but Barabbas." For the chief priests had stirred up the multitude to ask for Barabbas. Now Barabbas was a robber, and notorious prisoner. He had been imprisoned with the insurrectionists who had committed murder. While Pilate was sitting on the judgment seat, his wife sent to him, saying, "Have nothing to do with that righteous Man for last night I suffered greatly in a dream because of Him." Pilate was saying to them, "Then what shall I do to Him whom you call the King of the Jews?" And they shouted back, "Crucify Him!" Pilate was saying to them, "Why, what evil has He done?" But they shouted all the more, "Crucify Him!" Wishing to satisfy the multitude, Pilate released Barabbas for them. When Pilate saw that he was accomplishing nothing, but rather that a riot was starting, he took water and washed his hands in front of the multitude, saying, "I am innocent of this Man's blood; see to that yourselves." All the people answered and said, "His blood be on us and on our children!"

Pilate took Jesus, and scourged Him. Then the soldiers of the governor took Jesus into the Praetorium and gathered the whole Roman cohort around Him. They stripped Him, and put a scarlet robe on Him. After weaving a crown of thorns, they put it on His head, and a reed in His right hand, and they kneeled down before Him and mocked Him saying, "Hail, King of the Jews!" They spat on Him, and took the reed and began to beat Him on the head. Pilate came out again, and said to them, "Behold, I am bringing Him out to you, that you may know that I find no guilt in Him." Jesus came out, wearing the crown of thorns and the purple robe. Pilate said to them, "Behold, the Man!" When the chief priests and the officers saw Him, they cried out, saying, "Crucify, crucify!" Pilate said to them, "Take Him yourselves, and crucify Him for I find no guilt in Him." The Jews answered him, "We have a law, and by the law He ought to die because He made Himself out to be the

Son of God." When Pilate heard this statement, he was the more afraid; and he entered into the Praetoroum again, and said to Jesus, "Where are You from?" But Jesus gave him no answer. Pilate said to Him, "You do no speak to me? Do You not know that I have authority to release You, and I have authority to crucify You?" Jesus answered, "You would have no authority over Me, unless it had been given you from above; for this reason he who delivered Me up to you has the greater sin." As a result of this Pilate made efforts to release Him, but the Jews cried out, saying "If you release this Man, you are no friend of Caesar; every one who makes himself out to be a king opposes Caesar." When Pilate heard these words, he brought Jesus out, and sat down on the judgment seat at a place called The Pavement, but in Hebrew, Gabbatha. Now it was the day of preparation for the Passover; it was about the sixth hour. He said to the Jews, "Behold, your King!" They cried out, "Away with Him, crucify Him!" Pilate said to them, "Shall I crucify you King?" The chief priests answered, "We have no king but Caesar." So he then delivered Him up to them to be crucified.

CHAPTER FIFTY SEVEN

When Judas, who had betrayed Him, saw that He had been condemned, he felt remorse and returned the thirty pieces of silver to the chief priests and elder, saying, "I have sinned by betraying innocent blood." But they said, "What is that to us? See to that yourself!" He threw the pieces of silver into the sanctuary and departed; he went away and hanged himself. The chief priests took the pieces of silver and said, "It is not lawful to put them into the temple treasury, since it is the price of blood." They counseled together and with the money bought the Potter's Field as a burial place for strangers. For this reason the field has been called the Field of Blood to this day. Then that which was spoken through Jeremiah the prophet was fulfilled, saying, "And they took the thirty pieces of silver, the price of the one whose price had been set by the Sons of Israel; and they gave them for Potter's Field, as the Lord directed me."

Chapter Fifty Eight

They mocked Him, they took His robe off, put His garments on Him, and led Him away to crucify Him. As they were coming out, they pressed into service a passerby coming from the country, certain Cyrenian named Simon (the father of Alexander and Rufus), and placed on him the cross to carry behind Jesus. They came to a place called Golgotha, which means Place of a Skull.

There were following Him a great multitude of the people, and of women who were mourning and lamenting Him. But Jesus turning to them said, "Daughter of Jerusalem, stop weeping for Me, but weep for yourselves and for your children. For behold, the days are coming when they will say, 'Blessed are the barren, and the wombs that never bore, and breasts that never nursed.' Then they will begin to say to the mountains, 'Fall on us,' and the hills, 'Cover us.' For if they do these things in the green tree, what will happen in the dry?"

They crucified Him, and with Him two other men, (who were criminals, to be put to death) one on either side, and Jesus in between. The Scripture was fulfilled which says, "And He was reckoned with transgressors." Pilate wrote an inscription also, and put it on the cross. It was written, "JESUS THE NAZARENE, THE KING OF THE JEWS." Many of the Jews read this inscription, for the place where Jesus was crucified was near the city; and it was written in Hebrew, Latin, and in Greek. So the chief priests of the Jews were saying to Pilate, "Do not write, "The King of Jews'; but that He said, 'I am King of the Jews.'" Pilate answered, "What I have written I have written."

It was the third hour when they crucified Him. The soldiers, when they had crucified Jesus, took His outer garments and made four parts, a part to every soldier and also the tunic; now the tunic was seamless, woven in one piece. They said to one another, "Let us not tear it, but cast lots for it, to decide whose it shall be;" that the Scripture might be fulfilled, "They divided My outer garments among them, and for My clothing they cast lots." But Jesus was saying, "Father forgive them; for they do not know what they are doing." Sitting down, they began to keep watch over Him there

Those who were passing by were hurling abuse at Him, wagging their heads, and saying, "You who were going to destroy the temple and rebuild it in three days, save Yourself! If You are the Son of God, come down from the cross." In the same way the chief priests, along with the scribes and elders, were mocking Him, and saying, "He saved others; He cannot save Himself. He is the King of Israel; let Him now come down from the cross, and we shall believe in Him. He trusts in God; let Him deliver Him now, if He takes pleasure in Him; for He said, "I am the Son of God.'"

One of the criminals who were hanged there was hurling abuse at Him, saying, "Are you not the Christ? Save Yourself and us!" But the other answered, and rebuking him, said, "Do you not even fear God, since you are under the same sentence of condemnation?

We indeed justly, for we receiving what we deserve for our deeds; but this man had done nothing wrong." And he was saying, "Jesus, remember me when you come in Your kingdom!" He said to him, "Truly I say to you, today you shall be with Me in Paradise."

There were standing by the cross of Jesus, His Mother, and His Mother's sister, Mary the wife of Clopas, and Mary Magdalene. When Jesus saw His Mother, and the disciple whom He loved standing nearby, He said to His Mother, "Woman, behold, your son!" Then He said to John, "Behold, your Mother!" And from that hour the disciple took her into his own household.

CHAPTER FIFTY NINE

When the sixth hour had come, darkness fell over the whole land until the ninth hour. At the ninth hour Jesus cried out with a loud voice, "Eloi, Eloi, lama sabachthani?" which is translated, "My God, My God, why hast Thou forsaken Me?" When some of the bystanders heard it, they began saying, "Behold, He is calling for Elijah." After this, Jesus knowing that all things had already been accomplished, in order that the Scripture might be fulfilled, said, "I am thirsty." Someone ran and filled a sponge with sour wine, put it on a branch of hyssop, and brought it to His mouth, but He would not take it. The crowd was saying, "Let us see whether Elijah will come to take Him down." Jesus uttered a loud cry, and said, "It is finished! Father, into Thy hands, I commit My spirit." And breathed His last.

Behold, the veil of the temple was torn in two from top to bottom, the earth shook, the rocks were split, the tombs were opened; and many bodies of the saints who had fallen asleep were raised; coming out of the tombs after His resurrection they entered the holy city and appeared to many. Now the centurion, and those who were keeping guard over Jesus, when they saw the earthquake and the things that were happening, became very frightened and said, "Truly this is the Son of God! Certainly this man was innocent," and began praising God. All the multitudes who came together for this spectacle, when they observed what had happened, began to return, beating their breasts. All His acquaintances, were standing at distance, seeing these things. There were also some women looking on from afar, among whom were Mary Magdalene, and Mary the mother of James, Jess, Joses, and Salome.

When He was in Galilee, they used to follow Him and minister to Him; and there were many other women who had come up with Him to Jerusalem.

The Jews, because it was day of preparation, so that the bodies should not remain on the cross on the Sabbath (for the Sabbath was a high day), asked Pilate that their legs might be broken, and that they might be taken away. The soldiers came, and broke the legs of the first man, and of the other man who was crucified with Him; but coming to Jesus, when they saw that He was already dead, they did not break His legs; but one of the soldiers pierced His side with a spear, and immediately there came out blood and water. He who has seen has borne witness, and his witness is true; and he knows that he is telling the truth, so that you also may believe. For these things came to pass, that the Scripture might be fulfilled, "Not a bone of His shall be broken." Again another Scripture says, "They shall look on Him whom they pierced."

After these things Joseph of Arimathea, who was a prominent member of the Council, a good and righteous man, who was waiting for the kingdom of God; being a disciple of Jesus, but a secret one, for fear of the Jews, gathered up courage and asked Pilate that he might take away the body of Jesus. Pilate wondered if He was dead by this time, and summoning the centurion, he questioned him as to whether He was already dead. Ascertaining this from the centurion, he granted the body to Joseph. He came and took away His body. Nicodemus came also, who had first come to Him by night; bringing a mixture of myrrh and aloes, about a hundred pounds weight. So they took the body of Jesus, and bound it in linen wrappings with the spices, as is the burial custom of the Jews. Now in the place where He was crucified there was a garden; and in the garden a new tomb, in which no one had yet been laid. The tomb had been hewn out in the rock. On account of the Jewish day of preparation, because the tomb was nearby, they laid Jesus there. They rolled a stone against the entrance of the tomb. Now the women who had come with Him out of Galilee followed after, and saw the tomb and how His body was laid. They prepared spices and perfumes, but on the Sabbath they rested according to the commandment.

SATURDAY

Now on the next day, which is the one after the preparation, the chief priests and the Pharisees gathered together with Pilate, and said, "Sir, we remember that when He was still alive that deceiver said, 'After three days I am to rise again.' Therefore, give orders for the grave to be made secure until the third day, lest the disciples come, steal Him away and say to the people, 'He has risen from the dead,' and the last deception will be worse than the first." Pilate said to them, "You have a guard; go, make it as secure as you know how." And they went and made the grave secure, and along with the guard they set a seal on the stone.

CHAPTER SIXTY

SUNDAY

N ow as it began to dawn toward the first day of the week, Mary
Magdalene and the other Mary came to the grave, with spices,
that they might come and anoint Him. They were saying to one another,
"Who will roll away the stone for us from the entrance of the tomb?"
Behold, a severe earthquake had occurred, for an angel of the Lord
descended from heaven, came and rolled away the stone, although it
was extremely large, and sat upon it. His appearance was like lighting,
his garment as white as snow; the guards shook for fear of him, and
became like dead men. The angel answered and said to the women, "Do
not be afraid; for I know that you are looking for Jesus who has been
crucified. Why do you seek the living One among the dead? He is not
here, for He has risen, just as He said. That the Son of Man must be
delivered into the hands of sinful men, be crucified, and the third day
rise again. Come, see the place where He was lying. Go quickly and tell
His disciples that He has risen from the dead; and behold, He is going
before you into Galilee, there you will see Him; behold, I have told you."
They remembered His words. They went out and fled from the tomb,
for trembling and astonishment had gripped them. Returning from the
tomb, they reported all these things to the eleven and to all the rest.
They said, "They have taken away the Lord out of the tomb, and we do
not know where they have laid Him." Peter went forth, and the other
disciple, and they were going to the tomb. Two were running together;
and the other disciple ran ahead faster than Peter, came to the tomb

first; and stooping and looking in, he saw the linen wrappings lying there; but he did not go in. Peter also came, following him, entered the tomb; and he behold the linen wrappings lying there, and face cloth, which had been on His head, not lying with the linen wrappings, but rolled up in a place by itself. Then entered in, the other disciples also, who had first come to the tomb, he saw, and believed. For as yet they did not understand the Scripture, that He must rise again from the dead. So the disciples went away again to their own homes.

Mary was standing outside the tomb weeping; and as she wept, she stooped and looked into the tomb; and she beheld two angels in white sitting, one at the head, and one at the feet, where the body of Jesus had been lying. They said to her, "Woman, why are you weeping?" She said to them, "Because they have taken away my Lord, and I do not know where they have laid Him." When she had said this, she turned around, and behold Jesus standing there, and did not know that it was Jesus. Jesus said to her, "Woman, why are you weeping? Whom are you seeking?" Supposing Him to be the gardener, she said to Him, "Sir, if you carried Him away, tell me where you have laid Him, and I will take Him away." Jesus said to her, "Mary!" She turned and said to Him in Hebrew, "Rabbi!" (which means, teacher). Jesus said to her, "Stop clinging to Me; for I have not yet ascended to the Father; but go to My brethren, and say to them, 'I ascend to My Father and your Father, and My God and your God.'" Mary came, announcing to the disciples, "I have seen the Lord," and that He had said these things to her.

Some of the guards came into the city, and reported to the chief priests all that had happened. When they had assembled with the elders and counseled together, they gave a large sum of money to the soldiers, and said, "You are to say, 'His disciples came by night and stole Him away while we were asleep.' If this should come to the governor's ears, we will win him over and keep you out of trouble." They took the money and did as they had been instructed; and this story was widely spread among the Jews, and is to this day.

CHAPTER SIXTY ONE

N ow two of His disciples were going that very day to a village
named Emmaus, which was about seven miles from Jerusalem.
They were conversing with each other about all these things which
had taken place. It came about that while they were conversing and
discussing, Jesus Himself approached, and began traveling with them.
But their eyes were prevented from recognizing Him. He said to them,
"What are these words that you are exchanging with one another as
you are walking?" They stood still, looking sad. One of them, named
Cleopas, answered and said to Him, "Are You the only one visiting
Jerusalem unaware of the things which have happened here in these
days?" He said to them, "What things?" And they said to Him, "The
things about Jesus the Nazarene, who was a prophet mighty in deed
and word in the sight of God and all the people, and how the chief
priests and our rulers delivered Him up to the sentence of death, and
crucified Him. But we were hoping that it was He who was going to
redeem Israel. Indeed, besides all this, it is the third day since these
things happened. But also some women among us amazed us. When
they were at the tomb early in the morning, and did not find His body,
they came, saying that they had also seen a vision of a angel, who said
that He was alive. Some of those who were with us went to the tomb
and found it just exactly as the women also had said; but Him they did
not see." He said to them, "O foolish men and slow of heart to believe
in all that the prophets have spoken! Was it not necessary for the Christ
to suffer things and to enter into His glory?" And beginning with Moses
and with all the prophets, He explained to them the things concerning

Himself in all the Scriptures. They approached the village where they were going, and He acted as though he would go farther. They urged Him, saying "Stay with us, for it is getting toward evening, and the day is now nearly over." He went in to stay with them. It came about that when He had reclined at table with them, He took the bread and blessed it, and breaking it, He began giving it to them. Their eyes were opened and they recognized Him; and He vanished from their sight. They said to one another, "Were not our hearts burning within us while he was speaking to us on the road, while He was explaining the Scriptures to us?" They arose that very hour and returned to Jerusalem, and found gathered together the eleven and those who were with them, saying, "The Lord has really risen, and has appeared to us." They began to relate their experiences on the road and how He was recognized by them in the breaking of the bread.

While they were telling these things, He Himself stood in their midst. The doors were shut where the disciples were, for fear of the Jews. They were startled and frightened and thought that they were seeing a spirit. Jesus came and stood in the midst, and said to them, "Peace be with you. Why are you troubled, and why do doubts arise in you hearts? See My hands and My feet, that it is I Myself; touch Me and see, for a spirit does not have flesh and bones as you see that I have." When He had said this, He showed them His hands, feet and side. The disciples rejoiced when they saw the Lord. While they still could not believe it for joy and were marveling, He said to them, "Have you anything here to eat?" They gave Him a piece of a broiled fish; and He took it and ate it in their sight. Jesus said to them again, "Peace be with you; as the Father has sent Me, I also send you." When He has said this, He breathed on them, and said to them, "Receive the Holy Spirit. If you forgive the sins of any, their sins have been forgiven them; if you retain the sins of any, they have been retained." But Thomas, one of the twelve, called Didymus, was not with them when Jesus came. The other disciples were saying to him, "We have seen the Lord!" But he said to them, "Unless I shall see in His hands the imprint of the nails, and put my finger into the place of the nail, and put my hand into His side, I will not believe."

After eight days again His disciples were inside, and Thomas with them. Jesus came, the doors having been shut, and stood in their midst, and said, "Peace be with you." Then He said to Thomas, "Reach here your finger, and see My hands; and reach here your hand, and put it into My side; and be not unbelieving, but believing." Thomas answered and said to Him, "My Lord and my God!" Jesus said to him, "Because you have seen Me, have you believed? Blessed are they who did not see, and yet believed."

After these things Jesus manifested Himself again to the disciples at the Sea of Tiberias; and He manifested Himself in this way. There were together Simon Peter, Thomas called Didymus, Nathanael of Cana in Galilee, the sons of Zebedee, and two others of His disciples. Simon Peter said to them, "I am going fishing." They said to him, "We will also come with you." They went out, and got into the boat; and that night they caught nothing. But when the day was now breaking, Jesus stood on the beach; yet the disciples did not know that it was Jesus. Jesus said to them, "Children, you do not have any fish, do you?" They answered Him, "No." He said to them, "Cast the net on the right hand side of the boat, and you will find a catch." They cast, and then they were not able to haul it in because of the great number of fish. That disciple whom Jesus loved said to Peter, "It is the Lord." So when Peter heard that it was the Lord, he put his outer garment on (for he was stripped for work.), and threw himself into the sea. But the other disciples came in the little boat, for they were not far from the land, but about one hundred yards away, dragging the net full of fish. So when they got out upon the land, they saw a charcoal fire already laid, and fish placed on it, and bread. Jesus said to them, "Bring some of the fish which you have now caught." Peter went up, and drew the net to land, full of large fish, a hundred and fifty three; and although there were so many, the net was not torn. Jesus said to them, "Come and have breakfast." None of the disciples ventured to question Him, "Who are You?" Knowing that it was the Lord. Jesus came and took the bread, and gave them, and the fish likewise. This was the third time that Jesus was manifested to the disciples, after He was raised from the dead. So when they had finished breakfast, Jesus said to Simon Peter, "Simon, son of John, do you love

Me more than these?" He said to Him, "Yes, Lord; You know that I love You." He said to him, "Tend My lambs." He said to him again a second time, "Simon, son of John, do you love Me?" He said to Him, "Yes, Lord; You know that I Love You." He said to him, "Shepherd My sheep." He said to him the third time, "Simon, son of John, do you love Me?" Peter was grieved because He said to him the third time, "Do you love Me?" And he said to Him, "Lord, You know all things; You know that I love You." Jesus said to him, "Tend My sheep. Truly, truly, I say to you, when you were younger, you used to gird yourself, and walk wherever you wished; but when you grow old, you will stretch out your hands, and someone else will gird you, and bring you where you do not wish to go." Now this He said, signifying by what kind of death he would glorify God. When He had spoken then, He said to him, "Follow Me!" Peter turning around, saw the disciple whom Jesus loved following them; the one who also had leaned back on His breast at the supper, and said, "Lord, who is the one who betrays You?" Peter seeing him said to Jesus, "Lord, and what about this man?" Jesus said to him, "If I want him to remain until I come, what is that to you? You follow Me!" This saying went out among the brethren that that disciple would not die: yet Jesus did not say to him that he would not die, but only, "If I want him to remain until I come, what is that to you?"

CHAPTER SIXTY TWO

To these He also presented Himself alive, after His suffering, by many convincing proofs, appearing to them over a period of forty days, and speaking of the things concerning the kingdom of God. He gathered them together. He led them out as far as Bethany, now He said to them, "These are My words which I spoke to you while I as still with you, that all things which are written about Me in the Law of Moses and the Prophets and Psalms must be fulfilled." He opened their minds to understand the Scriptures, and He said to them, "Thus it is written, that the Christ should suffer and rise again from the dead the third day; and that repentance for forgiveness of sins should be proclaimed in His name to all the nations beginning from Jerusalem. You are witnesses of these things. And behold, I am sending forth the promise of My Father upon you; but you are to stay in the city until you are clothed with power from on high. John baptized with water, but you shall be baptized with the Holy Spirit not many days from now." He lifted up His hands and blessed them. He said to them, "All authority has been given to Me in heaven and on earth. Go into all the world and preach the gospel to all creation. He who has believed and has been baptized shall be saved; but he who has disbelieved shall be condemned. And these signs will accompany those who have believed; in My name they will cast out demons, they will speak with new tongues; they will pick up serpent, and if they drink any deadly poison, it shall not hurt them; they will lay hands on the sick, and they will recover." They were asking Him, saying, "Lord, is it at this time You are restoring the kingdom of Israel?" He said to them, "It is not for you to know times or epochs which the Father has fixed by His own authority; but you shall receive power when the Holy Spirit has come upon you; and you shall be My witnesses both in Jerusalem, and in all Judea and Samaria, and even to the remotest part of the earth. Now go and make disciples of all the nations, baptizing them in the name of the Father and the Son and the Holy Spirit teaching them to observe all that I commanded you; and lo, I am with you always, even to the end of the age." So then, when the Lord Jesus had spoken to them, He was lifted up while they were looking on, and a cloud received Him out of their sight. He was received up into heaven, and sat down at the right hand of God. As they were gazing intently into the sky while He was departing, behold, two men in white clothing stood beside them; and they also said, "Men of Galilee, why do you stand looking into the sky? This Jesus, who has been taken up from you into heaven, will come in just the same way as you have watched Him go into heaven." And they went out and preached throughout the world.

Epilogue

When the day of Pentecost had come, they were all together in one place. Suddenly there came from heaven a noise like a violent, rushing wind, and it filled the whole house where they were sitting. There appeared to them tongues as of fire distributing themselves, and they rested on each one of them. They were all filled with the Holy Spirit. As Jesus had told them of.

This is the disciples who bears witness of these things, and wrote these things; and we know that their witness is true. Many other signs, Jesus also performed in the presence of the disciples, (which if they were written in detail, We suppose that even the world itself could not contain the books which were written); which are not written in this book; but these have been written that you may believe that **Jesus is the Christ, the Son of God; and that believing you may have life in His name.**